CW00548561

"At last, a clear and lucid expositi‹
2023 and Synodality ⌐. _

FINOLA BRUTON
Chair, Dunboyne/Kilbride Pastoral Council and Member of the Irish
Episcopal Conference's Council for Marriage & The Family

* * *

"Do you feel that the church is at a crossroads? I do. If the church does not change gears now, then it will continue its backward slide into its own swamp of irrelevance. This book is about rescuing the church from that disaster, about pursuing the new course that Pope Francis is offering, where the church journeys forward with a much more engaged trajectory. That trip is called becoming a synodal church and you need to know about it so as to help get the church onto a whole new track now. Kudos to the editors who lay out a superb road map. Welcome aboard!"

JAMES F. KEENAN, S.J.
Canisius Professor, Boston College

* * *

"Written by experts in the field, this book provides an excellent and in-depth resource for understanding what it means to be a synodal church, how it can unfold and impact the mission of the church in Ireland and, yes, the entire church. Congratulations to the editors and authors for such a fine book."

DR MYRIAM WIJLENS
Prof. of Canon Law, University of Erfurt and Consultor to the Synod of Bishops

* * *

"Synodality promises to give voice and a hearing to all the baptized, enabling the Church to do better what it is doing right and to put right what it is doing wrong. This book is an excellent resource by a most credible and competent group of contributors toward such a vision for the Irish Church and (then to) the world."

DR THOMAS GROOME
Professor of Theology and Religious, Boston College

THE
SYNODAL
PATHWAY

WHEN **RHETORIC**
MEETS **REALITY**

EDITED BY
EAMONN CONWAY,
EUGENE DUFFY & MARY MCDAID

columba
BOOKS

First published in 2022 by

columbaBOOKS

Unit 3b Block 3, Bracken Business Park,
Bracken Road, Sandyford,Dublin 18, D18 K277
www.columbabooks.com

ISBN: 978-1-78218-393-8

Set in Adobe Garamond Pro 11/14 and Raleway Font Family
Cover and book design by Alba Esteban | Columba Books

Printed by SprintPrint, Ireland

EDITORS

EAMONN CONWAY is a priest and professor of theology at Mary Immaculate College in Limerick.

EUGENE DUFFY is a priest and theologian serving as Episcopal Vicar for Pastoral Renewal in the diocese of Achonry.

MARY MCDAID, Head of Pastoral Programmes at St Patrick's Sanctuary, Lough Derg, Co Donegal. Previously she worked as a secondary teacher in Catholic schools in Northern Ireland.

CONTENTS

SECTION 2. THE PRACTICE OF SYNODALITY

INTRODUCTION

On 10 March 2021, the Irish Catholic Bishops' Conference announced a Synodal Pathway for the Catholic Church in Ireland in preparation for a National Synodal Assembly or Assemblies within the next five years. This process focuses on the question: What does God want from the Church in Ireland at this time? Later in the same year, on 10 October 2021, Pope Francis launched a two-year global consultation process leading up to the XVI Ordinary General Assembly of the Synod of Bishops, dedicated to the theme, 'For a Synodal Church: Communion, Participation, and Mission'. This is to take place in Rome in October 2023. Opportunities for reflection and discussion as part of the global consultation are now meant to be underway in every diocese throughout the world, utilising documentation and online toolkits provided by the Holy See in the Autumn of 2021. Here in Ireland, in addition to participation in this global process, widespread consultations are also meant to be currently happening in parishes and dioceses specifically regarding the Synodal Pathway for the Irish Church.

The concept of synodality and the convening of synods is nothing new in the Catholic Church, yet recent focus upon it nationally and globally has taken many priests and people by surprise. Even after a year of launches, conferences, talks, homilies, pastoral letters, scholarly articles and popular social media contributions, there remains confusion and not an inconsiderable degree of concern regarding synodality. Without in many instances a proper understanding of what it is actually about, some people are already anxious that synodality will go too far in terms of demanding Church reforms while others are equally concerned that it will not go far enough.

This book is not setting out to allay people's fears. In fact, it may well do the opposite. Instead, it sets out to achieve three objectives. The first objective is to provide a basic understanding of the meaning of synodality and its rich foundations within the Catholic tradition. The second objective is to make the case for synodality as precisely 'that which God expects of the Church of the third millennium' (Pope Francis, 17th October 2015). The third objective is to show why, having embarked the Church upon a synodal path nationally and globally, failure to arrive at the desired destination of sincere and meaningful Church reform may well leave the Catholic Church in a worse situation than if it had never embarked upon a synodal path in the first place. In other words, the third objective of this book is to make the point that the stakes are high and it is time to 'get real'. The Irish Church, for instance, has embarked upon a number of resource-intense high-profile projects in the past decade for which the People of God had to dig deeply in order to provide not only the financial resources but also the considerable pastoral energy required to make them happen. Years of work, much of it voluntary, and huge sums of money went in to hosting the Eucharistic Congress in 2012 and the World Meeting of Families, which included a papal visit in 2018. Yet, to speak boldly, it is difficult to identify any enduring benefit in terms of renewal of the Irish Church's pastoral life from these events. As Eugene Duffy points out in his contribution to this book, there have also been many synodal-type initiatives in dioceses and religious congregations all over Ireland, the long-term fruit of which in many instances has also proven difficult to discern. With ever declining energy both of clergy and laity and much depleted resources, the People of God will need some convincing that investing themselves in the process of synodality is going to make any real difference.

For synodality to make a real difference, Pope Francis tells us, all those interested and involved need to adopt two inner dispositions that will determine their outward behaviour. The first is that of *parrhesia*, a Greek word often translated as 'boldness', by which is meant a resolve to speak plainly and frankly, without holding back out of fear of disagreement or of criticism. The second disposition is to resolve to listen openly, honestly and with humility to all those involved; to be prepared to listen not just to the words being spoken but also to the heart that is speaking them. These dispositions, Pope Francis believes, open minds and hearts to the promptings of the Holy Spirit and allow for an authentic discernment of what the Spirit is saying to the Church (Rev 3:22). These dispositions also characterise the approach to service of the Church taken by the authors who have contributed to this volume.

The first part of the book explores the foundations for synodality in the Catholic Church. Eamonn Conway provides a basic introduction to the concepts of synod and synodality and shows how much the practice of synods has already changed under Pope Francis. The renowned author and biographer of Pope Francis, Austen Ivereigh, lays out Pope Francis's vision of a synodal Church and offers a critique of synodal processes already underway in Australia and Germany. Rafael Luciani, who is a close collaborator with the Latin American Bishops and the Italian theologian Serena Nocetti, situates the renewed focus upon synodality within the context of ongoing reception of the Second Vatican Council.

Sr Nathalie Becquart SMCJ (a key member of Pope Francis's team at the Synod of Bishops) explains why, for Pope Francis, clericalism is in his words 'a scourge' and obstacle to synodality. Jos Moons SJ deepens our understanding of the process of discernment, which is central to synodality, and Jessie Rogers unfolds for us how synodality and discernment were practised widely in the early Church.

In his essay, Gerry O'Hanlon SJ, who was one of the first theologians to call for a synod of the Irish Church, helps readers come to grips with what is meant by the difficult theological concept of the *sensus fidei* and the light this can throw upon contested issues, such as gender and the role of women in the Church.

The second part of this book is more a view from the ground, or the pew, so to speak. Eugene Duffy evaluates previous excursions along synodal pathways in the Irish context and weighs up the pros and cons of formal synods versus more loosely-structured assemblies and gatherings. The late Bernd Hagenkord SJ, who served as a spiritual guide to the German Synodal Pathway before he died last year, provides an account of what has been happening recently in the German Church. Similarly, Timothy

Costello SDB provides an account of the synodal path being taken in the Australian context. In both these countries, synodality has been embarked upon as a response to harsh public criticism of the Church by civil authorities in the wake of revelations of sexual abuse and its cover-up.

Limerick is the only diocese in Ireland to have held a formal synod since Vatican II and Eamonn Fitzgibbon provides an account of the challenges and opportunities encountered in the process. Two experienced pastoral workers involved in Church renewal on the ground in their dioceses, Janet Forbes and Maureen Kelly, reflect on what needs to happen practically if synodality is to take effect. Finally, the pivotal issue of synodality and accountability is the focus of chapters by Nuala O'Loan and Patrick Treacy, both of whom have put their expertise in legal matters and public life at the service of Church reform. Common to their chapters is the call for both clergy and laity to take seriously the need to be openly accountable for their actions if there is any hope of those in leadership in the Catholic Church recovering credibility whether internally or in the public square. Both their chapters also identify specific obstacles to accountability in canon law that need to be addressed. Patrick Treacy takes up Becquart's earlier critique of clericalism, arguing that it has its deepest roots in hierarchicalism, of which he gives some practical examples before pointing to marriage and the family as a seedbed for authentic synodality.

This book brings together expertise that is global and local, theological, pastoral, legal and practical, and offers it as a companion for those who wish to contribute to the synodal journeys and processes now underway here in Ireland and globally. Each chapter is provided with discussion questions that might be useful to pastoral groups who may wish to work together, to tease out the various points and positions being put forward and relate the contents to their own specific situations and needs.

The editors are very grateful to the contributors and to Columba Books for their co-operation, in bringing this volume to print and their patience with delays in finalising the manuscript due to the impact of Covid-19.

_____

Laying the Foundations for Synodality

1

SYNODS AND SYNODALITY: WHAT IS IT ALL ABOUT AND WHY DOES IT MATTER?

Eamonn Conway

Eamonn Conway is a priest of the archdiocese of Tuam and professor of theology at Mary Immaculate College – University of Limerick. A former president of the European Society for Catholic Theology, he was appointed as an expert adviser to the XIII Ordinary General Assembly of the Synod of Bishops on 'The New Evangelisation for the Transmission of the Christian Faith' in 2012 by Pope Benedict XVI. He writes mainly in the areas of Christian anthropology and Catholic education. In this essay he introduces the concepts of synods and synodality, outlines the basis in Vatican II for Pope Francis's reforms, and explains why they are necessary.

The words 'Synod' and 'synodality' have become synonymous with Pope Francis. No other pontificate since Vatican II has been so closely associated with these concepts or has given them as much profile and attention as he has. This essay sets out to provide a basic introduction to synods and synodality that will be developed in more detail in subsequent essays in the book. It will explore how these concepts have evolved under Pope Francis and present some reasons as to why these developments are necessary.

The Synod of Bishops

The Synod of Bishops refers first and foremost to a permanent institution and office established in 1965 by Pope Paul VI and only secondarily to the periodic assemblies of bishops that the General Secretariat organises. It is not part of the Roman Curia. It is an advisory body and purely consultative, existing to assist the Pope in governance while always subject to his authority. Pope Francis's pontificate has been a busy one for the Synod of Bishops. He has called the Synod of Bishops 'one of the most precious fruits of the Second Vatican Council'.[1] Accordingly, he has significantly expanded it and given increased prominence to its General Secretariat in Rome.

What is a Synod?

The word 'synod' comes from Greek and refers to an assembly or a meeting, or, more literally, to journeying a common path. It is analogous with 'council', which is its Latin counterpart. In the Catholic Church it has come to mean an assembly of bishops along with experts and advisers meeting together to advise the pope, or a similar event at diocesan or regional level established to advise local bishops.

Since coming into office in 2013, Pope Francis has held two ordinary general assemblies of the Synod of Bishops: one extraordinary general assembly and one special assembly. The first assembly he convoked took place in 2014, the year following his election, and was an extraordinary synod on 'The Pastoral Challenges of the Family in the Context of Evangelization'. Extraordinary Synods are relatively brief and small; generally, apart from experts and advisers, only one bishop from each episcopal conference throughout the world is in attendance.

1   Pope Francis, *Communio episcopalis* (2018), n. 1.

In contrast, ordinary general assemblies can involve thousands and are month-long events. The first of these under Pope Francis took place in 2015 on 'The Vocation and Mission of the Family in the Church and in the Contemporary World'. The topic was deliberately aligned with that of the extraordinary synod that preceded it in the previous year and facilitated the most widespread period of consultation on pressing pastoral matters the global Catholic Church had then seen since Vatican II. It was followed by the 2018 Ordinary General Assembly on 'Young People, Faith and Vocational Discernment' and in 2019 by a special assembly on the Pan-Amazonian Region.

Most recently, Pope Francis has convoked an ordinary general assembly of bishops on the topic of synodality itself. The exact title is: 'For a synodal Church – communion, participation, mission.' This will take place in October 2023, by which time what Austen Ivereigh has described as the largest ever popular process of participation and consultation in world history, underway since October 2021, will have concluded. The consultation is intended to shape and influence the agenda that the assembly of bishops in synod will discuss. Essentially, synods are meant to be prayerful events during which, through honest and courageous speaking, and open, authentic listening (see Introduction) the will of the Holy Spirit can come to be revealed. Synods are not parliaments, as Pope Francis has clarified on more than one occasion, and they really don't have a secular equivalent.[2] This leaves the unique concept of a synod in the Catholic Church readily open to misunderstanding.

Was reform of the Synod of Bishops needed?

I can address this question with first-hand experience. Ten years ago (in 2012), I participated in the XIII Ordinary General Assembly of the Synod of Bishops in Rome. The theme was 'The New Evangelisation for the Transmission of the Christian Faith'. We didn't know it at the time but this was already intended by Pope Benedict to be his final

---

2   Most recently to leaders of the French Catholic Action movement (13 January 2022). See https://www.thetablet.co.uk/news/14893/synod-is-not-aiming-for-parliament-style-consensus-says-pope\.

Synod and so he ensured that it focused on the primary concern of his pontificate, namely, the re-evangelisation of Europe. For Benedict, as evident from his famous Regensburg address (2006), the state of health of Christianity globally was dependent upon the wellbeing of Christianity in Europe. This was because of the decisive and irreplaceable 'inner rapprochement', as he saw it, between biblical faith and Greek philosophy. Yet Europe was now ravaged by secularism, which had resulted in the 'desertification' of its rich Christian heritage, massive decline in religious practice and widespread doctrinal relativism. John Paul II's decade of evangelisation leading up to the new millennium hadn't resulted in the resurgence of faith in Europe that the pontificate had hoped for. A new initiative was needed.

As advisers we were seated near the back of the synod hall and our task was to take note of the various contributions from the Synod Fathers (all bishops, apart from a handful of male religious superiors). We were required to identify similarities and differences in their presentations, report on emerging themes and topics of interest, and keep an eye out for any theological anomalies. As all contributions were scripted and, in effect, vetted in advance, it was largely a paper exercise. There was supposed time for 'free interventions' in the evenings, but they didn't come across as such. An American Benedictine who sat next to me summed up the experience well: it was like 'being on a transatlantic flight all day every day and you don't even get to choose the movie'. Early in the Synod, officials became concerned by bishops posting to social media from within the synod hall and so the internet was switched off, causing lengthy queues in nearby phone shops as Synod Fathers rushed out to buy data SIM cards for their iPads so they could keep posting to social media.

There were only three significant differences of opinion voiced during the Synod. The first concerned the ordering of the sacraments of initiation. Cardinal Oullet, widely believed to be representing the position of Pope Benedict, favoured returning to the traditional order of confirmation before communion and was challenged by the then-Archbishop of Washington and Relator for the Synod, Cardinal Wuerl, who, without denying the theological coherence of Cardinal Ouellet's position, nonetheless tactfully defended the pastoral usefulness of having a sacrament of initiation for celebration with older age-groups. The second difference of opinion was more serious because it had to do with power and authority, and it led to a last-minute compromise text being inserted overnight into the Synod's concluding document to placate an influential minority. The issue was the role of the new ecclesial movements and the level of oversight in their regard that should be afforded to diocesan bishops.

The third difference of opinion was in regard to catechists. During the Synod there were several calls, primarily from Latin America but also from other regions, for the establishment of the position of catechist as a stable ministry in the Church. However, these were countered by bishops who were concerned that the establishment of stable lay ministries could diminish the distinctiveness of the priesthood, and so a firm proposal in this regard didn't find its way into the final propositions. Just last year, in May 2021, Pope Francis formally instituted the ministry of catechist.

The small discussion groups which took place in the second half of the Synod were livelier than those on the synod floor though they too were also carefully managed. Nothing found its way back onto the general floor unless it fitted into what seemed to many of us relatively harmless and reflected already predetermined magisterial positions. Groups tended to 'elect' as their chair the most senior ecclesiastic present and generally members were careful in what they said. The few lay people participating had been carefully selected and, if anything, the bishops found themselves tempering the more extreme views of the laity present. For instance, in the group in which I participated one of the lay members lobbied repeatedly for the Synod on the New Evangelisation to make a clear headline statement reiterating the Church's teaching on artificial contraception. Cardinals Dolan and Pell, both members of the group, assured the lay member of their complete acceptance of the Church's teaching on this matter but also made clear, as diplomatically as they could, that a reiteration of the Church's teaching on artificial contraception couldn't be one of the main outcomes of a synod on evangelisation.

There were a few truly memorable contributions. In anticipation of the humbler magisterial tone the Church would adopt in *Amoris*

Laetitia the Archbishop of Manila, Luis Antonio Tagle urged the Church to '…learn the power of silence. Faced with sorrows, doubts and uncertainties of people we cannot pretend there are easy solutions'. To Tagle's surprise, on the last day of the Synod, Pope Benedict XVI named him a cardinal (he is now Prefect of the Congregation for the Evangelization of Peoples). Along similar lines, fellow Filipino, Archbishop Villegas, said that 'the Gospel can be preached to empty stomachs, but only if the stomach of the preacher is as empty as his parishioners'. Then-Archbishop of Canterbury, Rowan Williams, said that to proclaim the Gospel in today's culture, marked as it is by truncated understandings of what it is to live a human life, is simply to restore people's confidence that it is possible to be properly human. 'The humanizing enterprise will be empty,' he said, 'without the definition of humanity given in the Second Adam.' Equal to Williams in insight and intellect, Pope Benedict made just one short but profound intervention during the Synod, an apparently *ex tempore* meditation he led at Morning Prayer to do with the beauty of the Gospel and the enduring hunger in every human heart for its message.[3] Throughout the Synod there was hardly a better or more profound articulation of the task facing the Synod Fathers than Pope Benedict's beautiful words. Unfortunately, however, the way the Synod was conducted stifled any possibility of an imaginative or creative response surfacing to the question he had so articulately posed.

Meanwhile, as hundreds of bishops from all over the world deliberated on new strategies for evangelisation, a few hundred metres away from the synod hall, a governance catastrophe in the Church of unprecedented proportions in the modern era was continuing to unfold in the papal apartments and the secretariat of state. Earlier in the year, Pope Benedict's butler had been arrested for stealing confidential documents, but this was only the tip of the iceberg. Anxious to bring to light the full extent of wrongdoing, Pope Benedict had commissioned an investigation headed by Spanish cardinal, Julian Herranz, the text of which would land on his desk a few weeks after the Synod

---

3 https://www.vatican.va/content/benedict-xvi/en/speeches/2012/october/documents/hf_ben-xvi_spe_20121008_meditazione-sinodo.html. Accessed 12 September 2021.

had concluded in December of 2012. Although never published, its findings were to dominate the pre-conclave discussions between cardinals that would take place a few months later and cause them to seek out a pope they felt was up to the task of bringing about badly needed reform in governance in the Church at every level.

Self-evidently, at a key low point in the Church's post-Vatican II history, the Synod of Bishops, established by Pope Paul VI for the purpose of assisting the pontiff in church governance and of sharing the burden of this responsibility with the bishops as a universal body, was in effect, inconsequential, attending to matters far removed from the pressing and serious matters immediately affecting the Church.

Pope Francis takes over

Pope Francis wasn't at the 2012 Synod. Although he had reached the mandatory age at which a bishop has to submit his resignation, Cardinal Bergoglio was still Archbishop of Buenos Aires so he could have participated. We have good reason to presume that the Synod of Bishops as it then operated held little attraction for him. Used by then to the open debate, honest and self-effacing interventions from diverse voices and perspectives, and an underlying trust in the guidance of the Holy Spirit that characterised the synodal-type gatherings of the bishops of Latin American episcopal conferences (CELAM), it is likely that the carefully contrived Roman synods may even have scandalised Cardinal Bergoglio. Also, he could well have had little interest in a synodal agenda he viewed as primarily Eurocentric. In fact, Francis takes a view diametrically opposed to Benedict regarding the significance of Europe for the global Church by explicitly rejecting the expectation that 'peoples of every continent, in expressing their Christian faith (would) imitate modes of expression which European nations developed at a particular moment of their history'.[4]

Within months of the conclusion of the 2012 Synod, as we know, Benedict resigned and Francis became pope. The XIII World

4   Pope Francis, *Evangelii Gaudium* (2013), n. 118.

Synod of Bishops is the only synod since Vatican II that doesn't have a post-synodal exhortation. When Francis took over, apparently the preparation of a carefully crafted exhortation by the committee of bishops appointed for that purpose was well-advanced, but Francis scrapped it and substituted his own text, *Evangelii gaudium* (2013), which in effect is the charter for his pontificate. And with that, the prefix 'new' before 'evangelisation', which owed its origins to John Paul II, was consigned to the ecclesiastical history books. Instead, Pope Francis pointed the Church back to Paul VI's *Evangelii nuntiandi* (1976), which he referred to on three separate occasions in the first few months of his pontificate, describing it as 'containing words that are as timely as if they had been written yesterday', 'a very full text that has lost nothing of its timeliness', 'that basic point of reference which remains relevant', and to his mind 'the greatest pastoral document that has ever been written to this day'.[5] Straightforward and uncomplicated definitions of evangelisation soon started to appear on the *@pontifex* twitter account such as, 'What does 'evangelise' mean? To give witness with joy and simplicity to what we are and what we believe in'. The Latin American response to secularism is characterised more by a call to joyful witness than to glum jeremiads about desertification. During the 2012 Synod several Latin American bishops commented upon how bishops from Europe generally seemed tired and frustrated by comparison with themselves. In retrospect, we know that this is because the Latin American Church had set a new and invigorating course for itself at Aparecida in 2007, which was already bearing fruit.

Imbedding Synods within a Synodal Church

The Synod of Bishops is in need of reform and Pope Francis is attempting to do this by imbedding the synodal assemblies of bishops within an operative culture of synodality that characterises the mode of being of the Church as a whole. Collegiality among bishops, which is a shared spirit of communion and collaboration occasionally

---

5   https://www.catholicworldreport.com/2013/12/12/the-greatest-pastoral-document-that-has-ever-been-written/. Accessed Sept 12 2021.

expressing itself in synodal assemblies, is being situated within a wider and more fundamental ecclesial synodality. That is, the synodal journey of the pilgrim of God as they journey through history.[6]

Synodality describes a style that reveals itself in how the Church goes about its daily business and affairs, 'expressing her nature as the People of God journeying together and gathering in assembly, summoned by the Lord Jesus in the power of the Holy Spirit to proclaim the Gospel.'[7] In other words, synodality, if truly operative, shows itself in how as a Church we celebrate liturgy, run our schools, look after our finances, prepare people for the sacraments, enable and empower our pastoral and finance councils and so on. The era of clerical authoritarianism has had its day. Only by praying and working together in mutual respect as God's people, ordained and lay, and drawing upon our complimentary giftedness and charisms, will we be able to live out our mission as Christians in today's world. Synodality is operative when the fruits of our labours as the people of God are being harvested, when our collective experience of serving one another and our communities is being mined and is being permitted to influence the path through history that the Church takes.

Pope Francis insists that synodality is constitutive of the Church. It is not an add-on so that lay people can be drafted in to bolster a collapsing clerical caste. It flows from the recognition that each member of the Church has a unique and crucial role to play in its mission, unique gifts given by the Holy Spirit in baptism for the service of God's kingdom. To fulfil their role, the People of God must be given voice, listened to and be heard. Pope Francis is convinced that this style of governance is essential to the Church and is precisely that to which God is calling it in the twenty-first century. Here in Europe we are playing catch-up with other parts of the world that have made better progress than we have in shifting towards a synodal style of governance, in particular Pope Francis's native Latin America. After centuries of being a 'sending' Church, in terms of missionaries, models

6 See in particular Luciani and Nocetti's contribution to this volume on the shift from episcopal collegiality to collegial synodality to ecclesial synodality.
7 See the *Vademecum for the Assembly of Bishops in Synod 2023, 1.2.* https://www.synod.va/en/documents/vademecum.html. Accessed 4 September 2021.

and mindsets, Europe is now experiencing a mission in reverse, for which Latin America, under the influence of Pope Francis, is a source.

As a global Church we are being invited to discover, perhaps for the first time since the early decades of the Church, what it means for 'all who believed to be together and have all things in common' (Acts 2:44). Pope Francis is not imposing upon the Church some new understanding he has invented but rather paring away centuries of accretions that are stifling the proclamation of the Gospel, to disclose the Church's original nature as essentially synodal. He is inviting us to jettison clerical customs, structures and practices in regard to Church leadership and governance that we tend to take for granted as to how things have to be, but which in reality have no Gospel justification or mandate and never did. What he wants us to rediscover and place our confidence in is 'the action of the Spirit in the communion of the Body of Christ and in the missionary journey of the People of God'.[8]

Pope Francis has described the transformation that is required in terms of shifting from a pyramidal to a synodal Church:

> There is a pyramidal Church, in which what Peter says is done, or there is a synodal Church, in which Peter is Peter but he accompanies the Church, he lets her grow, he listens to her, he learns from this reality and goes about harmonising it, discerning what comes from the Church and restoring it to her.[9]

A synodal Church can only come to be if it is led by bishops, priests and deacons capable of providing a synodal style of leadership along the lines Francis has described here.

Legitimacy in Vatican II

Pope Francis is the first pope since the Second Vatican Council not to have participated in any of its sessions. Arguably, this has given him a

---

8   See 'Synodality in the life and mission of the Church', *The Holy See: Congregation for the Doctrine of the Faith* (2018).

9   See Interview with the Holy Father, 7 December 2016. https://press.vatican.va/content/salastampa/en/bollettino/pubblico/2016/12/07/161207a.html

freshness of perspective when it comes to determining the Council's legacy. As Massimo Faggioli has remarked, Francis's papacy marks 'a second reception… under the matrix of mercy' and a re-inculturation of the papacy in the global Church.[10] The legitimacy of the synodal path Pope Francis is urging us to take is found firstly in the Second Vatican Council's Constitution on the Church, *Lumen gentium,* specifically, in Chapter 2 'On the People of God', and in the fact that this chapter precedes treatment of the hierarchical structure of the Church and the role of the episcopate. More specifically still, Pope Francis points to one sentence that contains a concept that is quite significant but not self-evident to understand. Speaking last year to the Italian bishops, Pope Francis explained that: 'The Synod is nothing more than making explicit what *Lumen Gentium* says: The totality of God›s people, everything from the bishop down, is "*infallibile in credendo*" (infallible in belief), i.e. cannot be wrong.'[11]

Much theological ink still needs to be spilled in unpacking this statement. Nonetheless, Pope Francis is the first Pope since Vatican II that has required the Church to take seriously this key aspect of conciliar teaching.

However, there is more to be said about how the Second Vatican Council provides Pope Francis with a basis for a synodal Church. It is to be found not so much in the documents of the Council as in the process the Council adopted that resulted in them. With Pope Francis, emphasis on reception of the Council has shifted from content to process; reception involves not merely another reading of the conciliar texts in the light of changing circumstances but also includes the style of deliberation the Council adopted, the open and confident way it engaged with the pressing questions of the time in light of the Tradition. Francis is attempting to receive the process of the Council by imbedding synodality into the daily life of the Church. He sees the synodal way the Council approached challenges the Church was facing as just as important a legacy in charting the way forward as

10 Böttigheimer, Christoph; Dausner, René (Eds.) 2016: *VATICANUM 21, Die bleibenden Aufgaben des Zweiten Vatikanischen Konzils im 21. Jahrhundert.* Freiburg: Herder. 29, 31.

11 See Pope Francis, Address the 74th General Assembly of the Catholic Bishops' Conference of Italy, 24 May 2021.

the conciliar texts themselves. While the Council documents remain normative, they are necessarily limited in that they couldn't have anticipated the profound transformation, the change of epoch as Pope Francis has called it, affecting both people and the planet today. The most enduring legacy of the Council is therefore to be found in the way it modelled intense listening to the Holy Spirit by the global Church. The Council rediscovered that such listening to the Holy Spirit is constitutive of the Church's nature and intended it to endure after the Council through the institution of the Synod of Bishops by Pope Paul VI in 1965.

Some bishops attending the 2012 Synod had carried out formal consultations with the people of their dioceses before attending, but these were the exception. In order to embed processes of listening globally in the Church, Pope Francis has now formally mandated what he has already insisted upon in practice for each of the synods over which he has presided: widespread and meaningful consultation prior to all synodal assemblies of bishops.

> Even in the preparation of Synodal Assemblies, it is very important that consultation of all the particular Churches be given special attention ... the Bishops submit the questions to be explored in the Synodal Assembly to the priests, deacons and lay faithful of their Churches, both individually and in associations, without overlooking the valuable contribution that consecrated men and women can offer. Above all, the contribution of the local Church's participatory bodies, especially the Presbyteral Council and the Pastoral Council, can prove fundamental, and from here "a synodal Church can begin to emerge".[12]

Pope Francis has held several preparatory meetings with diverse groups in advance of each synod he has convoked. He has insisted upon various voices being heard within the synod hall. He has expanded the number of those other than bishops who can vote at synods. In these ways, he is seeking to embed synodal assemblies within

12   Pope Francis, *Episcopalis communio* (2018), n.7.

a synodal culture that is intended to embrace the Church as a whole. Peter is still Peter and bishops still bear the burden of decision-making, but they must do so while listening to and responding to the Holy Spirit revealing its will for the Church in the lives of all the faithful.

Conclusion

We shouldn't underestimate the conversion of mindset and mentalities that embracing synodality requires. There will be the temptation to embrace synodality only half-heartedly, to appear to go along with things until a new pontificate becomes preoccupied with different priorities.

Some will point to the fact that we have tried synodal-type processes in the Church in the past and that they failed, only serving to deepen disillusionment. Yet it is worth considering if this latest effort is different in that the ground is being better prepared and synodal events will no longer be isolated events in a wider Church culture that still goes about its business in a hierarchical and authoritarian manner.

There will be others in the Church who are quite comfortable with and personally invested in a hierarchical and authoritarian way of being Church. They may take the view that they have much to lose personally. However, this is not the case because that way of being Church simply has no future.

Instead, this is a time to trust, to hope, and to dream, or, as Pope Francis often urges us, to see, to judge and to act. Our planet, faced with an ecological crisis unthinkable before, needs the voice of a strong and vibrant Church to protect it. Our Church, faced with virtually a complete loss of credibility in several parts of the world, needs a form of governance that is healthy, mature and respectful of all.

Questions

- *'The era of clerical authoritarianism has had its day'. How can the synodal process ensure that the giftedness and charisms of all the people of God can be drawn upon to create a new style of governance in the church?*

- *We 'cannot underestimate the conversion of mindset and of mentalities that embracing synodality requires'. How might a diocese facilitate this conversion? What obstacles might be encountered in so doing and how might they be overcome?*

2

POPE FRANCIS'S VISION OF A SYNODAL CHURCH: THE SPIRIT IN THE ASSEMBLY

Austen Ivereigh

Austen Ivereigh is a writer and journalist, and the world's leading biographer on Pope Francis. In this chapter he demonstrates that the vision of the Francis pontificate is itself the fruit of a synodal process (the Latin American Bishops 2007 assembly at Aparecida, Brazil) and that the implementation and reinvigoration of synodality is one of its central aims. Dr Ivereigh summarises Francis's vision of synodality drawing on the Pope's own statements in *Let Us Dream* in order to note the tensions between that vision and various processes currently being implemented in local Churches, especially Germany and Australia.

Austen Ivereigh is a Fellow in Contemporary Church History at the Jesuit-run Campion Hall, University of Oxford and holds a D Phil (Oxon) for a thesis on Church and politics in Argentina.

A few months after his election in March 2013, Pope Francis recalled Cardinal Carlo Maria Martini's dream of a synodal Church, noting how long and difficult the cardinal knew the path to it would be. Francis said he wanted to proceed 'gently, but firmly and tenaciously' down that route.[13] He has been true to his word. The Francis pontificate has seen a springtime of synodality and its corollary, collegiality, as vital instruments for the keeping alive the experience of the Second Vatican Council.

Focusing firstly on regenerating the institution of the Synod of Bishops in Rome, established by Pope Paul VI in 1965 after centuries of disuse, Francis has regenerated it as an authentic mechanism of ecclesial discernment actively involving the People of God, while using the four synodal assemblies held in Rome in October (2014, 2015, 2018 and 2019) to teach and inspire the rest of the Church to do the same. Finally, at the start of the ninth year of his pontificate, on the eve of Pentecost 2021, he announced a global synodal process involving all the dioceses of the world, culminating in October 2023 with the XVI ordinary general assembly of the Synod of Bishops. It will be the most significant and far-reaching ecclesial event since the Second Vatican Council, embedding the Council permanently in the dynamic life of the Church, obviating, perhaps, the need for a future ecumenical council.

At the time of the announcement, national synodal 'processes' were already underway in Australia ('Plenary Council') and in Germany ('Synodal Way'), and preparations were being made in Ireland and in Italy. In Latin America, where the continental episcopal body CELAM is the only successful example worldwide of a regional Church with decades of practice in synodality, a continent-wide 'Ecclesial Assembly' was being held using a 'synodal' methodology of listening and participation.[14] A number of dioceses – in Ireland, Limerick; and the UK,

---

13 Interview, quoted in Austen Ivereigh, *The Great Reformer: Francis and the Making of a Radical Pope* (2014: New York, Henry Holt), 372.

14 For Australia, see https://plenarycouncil.catholic.org.au; for Germany, see (in English) https://www.synodalerweg.de/english; for Ireland, see Sarah MacDonald, 'Catholic bishops plan synod...in Ireland', *The Irish Independent*, 26 February 2021; for Latin America, see asambleaeclesial.lat. Also: Pope Francis address to national catechetical office of the Italian Bishops' Conference, 30 January 2021.

Liverpool – have recently concluded synodal processes, inspired by Francis's call for listening, dialogue and discernment at all levels to replace a clerical, self-referential institutional culture held responsible for dysfunction and scandal.[15]

Francis's stress on synodality has opened a new stage of the reception of Vatican II, marking the end of a thirty-year hegemony of communion ecclesiology following the synod of 1985 in which the full implications of the People of God in *Lumen Gentium* were downplayed by a papacy nervous of a hermeneutic of rupture. Synodality, for Francis, is the expression of the Church as polyhedron and inverted pyramid implied by *Lumen Gentium*, in which the People of God – the members of the Church, equal in dignity – are served by the hierarchy concerned for their *salus animarum*, their salvation and wellbeing, and are emboldened to go out in service of humanity.[16] Synodality, in Francis's regenerative conception, allows for the full ecclesiological consequences of the Church as the people of God, and is inextricably bound up with a call for a missionary, centrifugal Church, *ex natura ad extra*, in which ordinary believers take responsibility for evangelising our world as missionary disciples. This missionary impulse – 'so that the Church's customs, ways of doing things, times and schedules, language and structures can be suitably channeled for the evangelisation of today's world rather than for her self-preservation' in his famous phrase from *Evangelii Gaudium* (27) – calls for a Church in dialogue, both with the world and internally, in which the renewal of structures is implicit in a process of permanent pastoral conversion.

---

15 'On the one hand, we inherit from more than 1,500 years a hierarchical, clerical Church where the clerics are separated from the laity. On the other hand we can imagine a synodal Church as described by the Second Vatican Council but which has not yet been received and implemented … The synod could help us turn a clerical Church into a synodal Church.' Interview with Sr Nathalie Becquart, one of the undersecretaries for the office of the Synod of Bishops, *National Catholic Reporter*, 27 April 2020.

16 See Richard R. Gaillardetz, 'The "Francis Moment": a New Kairos for Catholic Ecclesiology,' *CTSA Proceedings* 69 (2014): 63-80. On Francis's 'papal populism', see Austen Ivereigh, '"We Belong to a People"', in Barbara E. Wall & Massimo Faggioli (eds.) *Pope Francis: A Voice for Mercy, Justice, Love and Care for the Earth* (New York: Orbis Books, 2019): 128-154.

This conversion in turn demands dialogue and discernment processes that open the centre to the periphery, pastoral practice to lived experience, the deductive to the inductive, involving the Church at every level, on the ancient principle of *Quod omnes tangit ab omnibus tractari debet*: what affects all should be discussed by all.[17] Francis invoked the phrase on 17 October 2015, in a speech that remains the magna carta of his vision for a synodal Church, to mark the 50th anniversary of the restoration of Synod of Bishops by Pope Paul VI. Francis described synodality in the strongest possible terms as a 'constitutive dimension of the Church' and 'what God expects of the Church of the third millennium' – some of the strongest words a pope can use.[18]

Yet, like early Spring in these islands, the new season of synodality has not been short of cold winds and surprise frosts. The two Rome synods on the family, of October 2014 and October 2015 especially, triggered intense debate and stirred powerful latent phobias across the conservative Catholic world that the Church was renouncing its commitment to the indissolubility of marriage. Although this was deeply untrue (both the synod final report and the post-synod exhortation *Amoris Laetitia* were focused on almost every page on enabling the Church to better help people to live indissolubility), the hysteria reflected in media reports distorted its reception, pushing many suspicious conservatives into a state of semi-schism and making discernment all but impossible. 'The effect was to reduce the spiritual freedom that is so vital in a synodal process,' Francis recalled in our book *Let Us Dream*. 'Each side, entrenched in "their" truth, ended up being imprisoned in their own positions.'[19]

The Amazonian synod of October 2019 also led to baseless accusations promoted by conservative Catholic media that paganism and syncretism had penetrated Catholicism in the guise of inculturation, vividly illustrating what in *Let Us Dream* the Pope calls 'the isolated

---

17   ee Gerry O'Hanlon SJ, *The Quiet Revolution of Pope Francis: A Synodal Church in Ireland?* (Dublin: Messenger Publications, 2019): 48-52.

18   Pope Francis, Address, Ceremony commemorating the 50th anniversary of the institution of the Synod of Bishops, 17 October 2015.

19   Pope Francis, *Let Us Dream. The Path to a Better Future*. In conversation with Austen Ivereigh (2020, New York/London: Simon & Schuster), 88.

conscience'.[20] Francis's response to the synod in his February 2020 exhortation, *Querida Amazonia*, was more likely to dismay progressives convinced that the majority vote at the synod in favour of ordaining married men and women deacons gave the Pope the legitimacy he needed to proceed with those reforms. When he chose not to implement the majority synod vote in favour of both measures, he was accused of caving to conservative pressure.[21]

A second challenge has been a 'functionalist' hermeneutic, especially in those Churches – both Australia and Germany are examples – recovering from devastating sex abuse crises that have thrown into doubt the Church's governance structures. The German Synodal Way is specifically in response to the devastating "MHG Study" of September 2018 conducted by an interdisciplinary consortium commissioned by the German bishops' conference, which reviewed case files of Catholic clergy over many decades. Even the topics of the three forums of the *Synodale Weg* – power, sexuality and clergy – were determined by the MHG report (a forum on women has since been added). The 'fundamental text' adopted by the *Synodale Weg* describes a 'synodal Church' as one that includes separation of powers, participation in decision-making and other elements of 'inculturation into democracy', which they say are vital for the credibility of the Church in democratic societies.[22] There is a clear tension between this 'German' version of synodality — one preoccupied with structural, functional, institutional reform — and Francis's conception, which starts with the mission ad gentes, and which puts listening to the people of God and discernment at its heart, as the Pope himself made clear in a concerned letter to the German Church.[23]

Such tensions are no surprise: Francis is asking the Church to embrace a *modus vivendi et operandi* that lies at the heart of its very self yet

20 *Let Us Dream*, 69-74.
21 See Massimo Faggioli, "The limits of a pontificate", 2-part critical article in *La Croix International*, 14-15 April 2020, and response by Pedro Gabriel, 'Faggioli and the limits of reform', *Where Peter Is*, 22 April 2020.
22 See *Der Synodale Weg*, 'Fundamental text' adopted 3 December 2020, at synodalerweg.de/english. See also report and reccommendations of church leaders in Australia, 'The Light from the Southern Cross', released 15 August 2020.
23 'Carta del Santo Padre al Pueblo de Dios que peregrina en Alemania', 29 June 2019.

with which it has become deeply unfamiliar. Even the task of reuniting in assembly, and in participating actively in the evangelising mission, is an experience alien to most of the faithful. Francis's repeated warnings against functionalism and focus on governance questions in synodal processes, and his insistence on the primacy of the Spirit – that is, in church reform, there is no good that can be accomplished *without* the mediation of the Spirit – has led even supportive voices to question whether Francis's understanding of synodality is more akin to the rarified practices of superiors of religious orders than to bishops.[24]

Yet in reality, his concern is above all to recapture the charismatic, dynamic and popular element of the early councils of the Church, an element best expressed in both the Jesuit tradition of apostolic discernment in common and in Latin America's history of general conferences since the 1950s. The Council of Jerusalem described in Acts of the Apostles chapter 15 involves the participation of 'the apostles, the elders, and the whole Church' (Acts 15:22) and ends with St Peter telling the assembly: 'It has seemed to the Holy Spirit and to us' (Acts 15:28). Both elements are key: the assembly of the people, and the prompting of the Spirit. In going to the heart of Francis's understanding of synodality, I want to argue for the importance of these two elements which, because they are often overlooked or downplayed in some European and American discussions of this topic, can lead to serious misreadings by both progressive and conservative Catholics.

The Latin American Episcopate's General Conference at Aparecida, Brazil, in May 2007, was prepared over many years by hundreds of 'mini synods' across the continent and became the deepest signs-of-the-times discernment undertaken by the Church in any part of the world in recent decades. It resulted in an extraordinary 'Pentecost' moment that invigorated the Latin-American Church's understanding of its mission in the contemporary era, whose concluding document was written under the supervision of then Cardinal Jorge Mario Bergoglio. The great notes of the Francis era —a merciful, joyful, Spirit-filled Catholicism that captivates by offering the experience of

---

24 Massimo Faggioli, 'Synod and Synodality in Pope Francis's Words', *The Way* (spirituality journal of the British Jesuits), Vol. 59, Number 4 (October 2020) 89-100, and 'Synodality and Papal Primacy', *La Croix International*, 27 April 2021.

the encounter with Christ; an outward-facing Church of service rooted in the People of God; a determination to reform in response to the ongoing conversion of a Church responding to the Spirit — were all first struck at Aparecida in the form of a coherent, symphonic whole. As the theologian Carlos Galli neatly puts it: 'Yesterday, Bergoglio gave us Aparecida; today, Aparecida gives us Francis.'[25]

The influence of the vision of the Aparecida document (DA) on the Francis pontificate is by now commonplace, not least because of its obvious influence on his programmatic 2013 exhortation, Evangelii Gaudium. Yet few have noted the way the Aparecida process has profoundly shaped Francis's pontificate. The 'programme' of DA flowed out of a process that began with asking how the Lord was calling on the Latin-American Church to evangelise in the new circumstances of the 'change of era' (cambio de época). This is the question with which Francis believes all synodal processes should begin, and from which reforms and pastoral priorities must flow.

The second essential element of Francis's synodality is its pneumatology. For Bergoglio, there is no true synodality without the action of the Spirit, which is detected in the movements, in consolations and desolations, and above all in the action he describes vividly in *Let Us Dream* as 'overflow'.[26] This action is one that is felt above all in contexts of tension and disagreement when the parties involved choose not to pursue by means of power the triumph of their own point of view, but rather agree to maintain in tension different views in expectation of an 'overflow' that will transcend the existing polarities, resolving them on a higher plane. Although Bergoglio's expression of this pneumatological phenomenon is original and profound – indeed, he brings to it a particular genius, the fruit of decades of blending Ignatian discernment with insights from Romano Guardini's understanding of generative disagreement – it is a mistake to dismiss this as a personal or idiosyncratic take. His understanding of the Spirit's action in the Church as a coincidentia oppositorum – the alchemy of a synod that creates a

---

25 Carlos Maria Galli, 'Revolución de la ternura y reforma de Iglesia', in Rafael Luciani y Carlos Schickendantz (coords), *Reforma de Estructuras y Conversión de Mentalidades: Retos y Desafíos para una Iglesia Sinodal* (Ed. Khaf, 2019), 49.

26 *Let Us Dream* 7, 21, 80-81.

reconciled diversity – powerfully re-articulates for our age the dynamic of early-Church discernment of the Spirit in the assembly.[27]

What Francis seeks to bring about in the global Church through the 2021-2023 global synodal process is not, in other words, a Latin-American program of reform, but the process that led to that reform, which each Church is called to make its own. It is a process that involves a return to the Church's own roots: apostolic discernment in common, rooted in the experience of the People of God, focused on mission and evangelisation. The synodal path, says Francis, begins in every Christian community, from the bottom up. It is not so much a program to be carried out or a decision to take but above all 'a style to incarnate', that is, 'dialogue, discussion, research – but with the Spirit'.[28]

The style of Aparecida is missionary in outlook, reading the spirits in the light of the signs of the times, and involving and oriented to the whole People of God, rather than elite groups. 'Synodality starts with hearing from the whole People of God,' Francis says in *Let Us Dream*, adding: 'A Church that teaches must be firstly a Church that listens.' As Cardinal Mario Grech, the synod secretary general, put it to the Irish bishops, 'synodality is not just a methodological choice, but the mode of being of a church which wants to go out in mission. Indeed, synodality is not only a *methodos* but an *odos*, not only a method but a way towards a re-thinking of the Church's role in contemporary society.' It is 'the particular style that characterises the life and mission of the Church, expressing her nature as the People of God journeying together and gathering in assembly, summoned by the Lord Jesus in the power of the Holy Spirit in order to proclaim the Gospel'.[29] This 'style' or way of proceeding is not just what suits the Church as a complex global institution, in other words, but a format that expresses its

---

27 On Francis's development of Guardini's theory of contraposition, see Massimo Borghesi, *The Mind of Pope Francis. Jorge Mario Bergoglio's Intellectual Journey* (trans. Barry Hudock, 2017: Collegeville, Minn.: Liturgical Press) chapter 3. The Pope also summarizes his understanding of contrapositions – and the Spirit's role in trascending them – in *Let Us Dream* 78-81.

28 Francesco, "Ai Membri del Consiglio Nazionale dell'Azione Cattolica Italiana" (30 April 2021).

29 'Towards a Synodal Irish Church. Address of Cardinal Mario Grech to the Bishops of Ireland', 3 February 2021.

very nature, allowing the Church to embody what it proclaims. 'The synodal order is a way of expressing the primacy of love at the level of the Church itself', as Ghislain Lafont puts it.[30]

The see-judge-act method of authentic synodality always starts with the experience of the People of God. In the Aparecida process, listening to the Spirit began long before the bishops met at the Brazilian shrine, in countless exercises in understanding the lives of ordinary people. Aparecida asked: what is happening, and what effect is it having on God's creation and His creatures, especially the poor and vulnerable? What factors, internal and external (and their interplay), lead the poor to cry out, and what factors prevent the Church bringing the Good News to them? How must the Church change to facilitate the mission in the changed context of today? How can the Church enable the encounter with Jesus Christ that changes our horizon?[31] The same pastoral-missionary hermeneutic underpins the Australian Plenary Council, which began with more than 200,000 Catholics gathering to answer the question: 'What is God asking of us in Australia at this time?' More than 17,000 summary responses were submitted, prior to the first assembly of the Plenary Council in October 2021, the first since the Second Vatican Council. Archbishop Mark Coleridge, Australian bishops' conference president, describes 'trying to hear the Spirit in the vast cacophony of the Church' as a 'slow, messy' process, but is the only path to 'a future worth happening'.[32]

Episcopalis Communio says the synod gives voice to the entire people of God via the bishops as authentic guardians, interpreters and witnesses of the faith of the whole Church. Yet even in the Synod of Bishops not only bishops are present and vote. Many priests, Religious, lay people, ecumenical delegates and so on take part in small-group discussions and address the assembly. Prior to the youth (2018) and

---

30 Ghislain Lafont, *Piccolo saggio sul tempo di papa Francesco: Poliedro emergente e piramide rovesciata*, Edizioni Dehoniane Bologna, 59.

31 On the Francis pontificate as the fruit of Aparecida, see Austen Ivereigh, 'Close and Concrete: Bergoglio's Life Evangelizing a World in Flux', in Brian Y. Lee and Thomas L. Knoebel (eds.) *Discovering Pope Francis: The Roots of Jorge Mario Bergoglio's Thinking* (Collegeville. Minn: 2019) 23-41.

32 As he told Christopher Lamb, 'Catholic Church must embrace "synodality"', *The Tablet*, 26 March 2021.

Amazonian (2019) synods were 'pre-synods' in which those directly involved – 35 young people in the first case, 17 representatives of native peoples in the second – were directly consulted and went on to play important roles in the synod process itself. At the Amazonian synod, the fruit of two years of local assemblies involving 60,000 people, indigenous leaders sat among the synod delegates, and were invited regularly to address the gathering. For Francis, the synod must be not just *for* the people, but *with* the people: hearing the Spirit call out to the Church through their experiences and needs.

In all four synods, the approach has been inductive and pastoral, adopting the hermeneutic of the missionary disciple and the Good Shepherd. It begins by looking outwards, to the reality of what *is*, and the desire to heal and to care for what is vulnerable or in pain. Thus, the centre (considered here as church leadership) opens to the periphery and allows itself to be affected and changed by what it sees. Then it moves to discernment: why is it this way? What is God's will for this situation? What needs to change (a) in the world, to conform it to Christ and God's Kingdom, and (b) in the Church, in order to enable that change? (In the (b) question, reform is a means to a pastoral end, not an end in itself; just as the Church does not exist for itself but as an agent of God's pastoral purpose.) The clarity gained in the discernment then guides the proposals for concrete action that conclude the synodal process. The emphasis is on renewal of the Church, understood not primarily in terms of structural reform, but rather of the *ressourcement* and *aggiornamento* that characterized Vatican II.

This dynamic is in the very DNA of the *ekklesia*, a body which is called out, formed and assembled, to hear the Spirit speak: in the Tent of Meeting in Exodus, the Council of Jerusalem in Acts, or in a papal conclave. Although for many centuries it was dragged in the direction of an imperial monarchy, and nowadays many want it to look like a constitutional democracy, the Church is neither monarchic nor democratic but synodal. For the Church to fail to embrace synodality is to submit to worldliness. Fear of change and contamination and a deep sense of threat have led the Church over time to abandon trust in the Spirit of the Assembly in favour of juridicism, moralism and rationalism, ironically emulating the modernity it claims to resist. This command-and-control Catholicism in turn provokes a search for reforms that borrow more from parliamentary systems than the Church's own tradition.

Both the conservative and progressive mindsets are inimical to synodality.

For *conservatives*, the primary preoccupation is not discerning God's will in the face of pastoral need but the need to stand up for the truth of the Catholic faith without compromise in the face of the threat of change. A synod in this thinking can never be more than a means of designing new reiterations of timeless truths and condemning fresh errors, even claiming that this modus operandi is 'pastoral' because it guides people in the way of truth. The Vatican's synod managers during the pontificates of St John Paul II and Benedict XVI operated on something close to the assumption that the clerical hierarchy was responsible for defending and teaching doctrine to the People of God, who were called to obey authorities that commanded unquestioning obedience. Even before the scandals, such a model was at odds with the ecclesiology of Vatican II; in their wake, it is unsustainable. Francis's four synods have clearly overturned that assumption, creating a dynamic of ecclesial discernment that, as the family synod followed by *Amoris Laetitia* showed, is clearly able to develop doctrine and the means of its application through a process that begins with consulting the faithful and involves the People of God at every stage. Seen through the conservative prism, this dynamic synodality raises fears of a Trojan horse concealing a plan to unravel tradition and to compromise with modernity – the very fear that led to synodality dying out in the Latin Catholic Church.[33]

---

33 On the previous model of synods, see my *The Great Reformer*, esp. Chapter 7, which tells how they were seen through Cardinal Bergoglio's eyes; and my *Wounded Shepherd: Pope Francis and His Struggle to Convert the Catholic Church* chapter 9, which shows how the 2014-15 family synod's method afforded the authentic discernment that was not possible at the synod of 2005. For a conspiratorial conservative view of the same synod see Ross Douthat, *To Change the Church: Pope Francis and the future of Catholicism* (2018: New York, Simon & Schuster) which is driven by a hermeneutic of suspicion. Douthat claims that for Francis and a small group of advisers the synod is a political instrument that allows them to push through liberalization of church doctrine in the face of a largely conservative episcopate.

Yet *progressives* have too often misinterpreted this more dynamic synodality under Francis as a reform of the Church's teaching and structures as its primary objective. Again, the hermeneutic assumption here needs to be exposed. Where for the conservative, the hermeneutic is driven by fear of change, the progressive hermeneutic is frustrated with Church traditions and teachings, which are seen as *per se* unjust and an obstacle to evangelisation because they are antithetical to modernity. Thus, the primary task of a synod in the progressive view is to dismantle those structures in order to make the Church more acceptable. The Pope's 2019 letter to the German Church reflects his concern at this hermeneutic, warning against the temptation to focus on a structural reorganisation that privileges the efforts and aptitudes of competing elite groups, distant from the concrete needs and experiences of ordinary people, 'revolving around a complex set of arguments, speeches and resolutions that do no more than remove us from real and daily contact with the faithful people and with the Lord.' He urges them instead to focus on the evangelisation question, asking what the Spirit asks of the Church and what gifts He is bestowing to enable them to respond to that call.[34]

The risk of Germany's Synodale Weg – which, unlike the Australian process, is not a canonical synod, but sui generis – is that it excludes discernment by a predetermined Pelagian program that focusses on the Church's own structures. The reforms of the Francis pontificate – the war on clericalism and corruption, the inculcation of a culture of service of humanity rather than a command-and-control mentality, the centrality of the poor, the emphasis on the experience of the encounter with a merciful God — are fruits of the Aparecida discernment, flowing from the recognition of how the Church can serve the needs of the people (especially the poor) at this time. They are a means to an end. The telos of a synod is not the Church, but humanity, just as the power to change the Church rests not with a program of reform but a conversion of mindset that is fruit of the action of the Spirit. As Pope Francis wrote to Cardinal Reinhard Marx in June 2021, refusing his resignation:

---

34 'Carta del Santo Padre al Pueblo de Dios que peregrina en Alemania', 29 June 2019.

It is the path of the Spirit we are to follow, and the starting point is humble confession: we have erred, we have sinned. We will not be saved by surveys nor by the power of institutions. We will not be saved by the prestige of our Church that tends to hide its sins; nor will we be saved by the power of money nor the opinion of the media (on which we are so often too dependent). What will save us is opening the door to the only One who can, and to confess our nakedness: "I have sinned", "we have sinned" … And to cry, to stammer as we can that "get away from me, for I am a sinner", a legacy that the first Pope left to the future popes and the bishops of the Church. And then we will feel that healing shame that opens the doors to the compassion and tenderness of the Lord who is always close to us. As a Church we must ask for the grace of shame, and for the Lord to save us from being the shameless prostitute of Ezekiel chapter 16.[35]

A synod is not a parliament or a committee of inquiry in which experts debate and discuss solutions to problems, but an act of collective discernment that opens the Church to the action of the Spirit. Francis points out that the first, twin synods of his pontificate, of October 2014 and October 2015 on marriage and family, did not gather 'to resolve' the question of access to Communion for the divorced and remarried, but rather to enable the Church better to support lasting marriages and strong families in a context where both had been weakened in culture and law. In order to tend to the wounded and to offer support to those who needed it, the Church needed to move beyond some of the casuistic thinking that had made it harder for the Church to support and guide people in complex, real-life situations. Yet both conservatives and progressives – feeding and at times fed by the media – framed the synod as 'about' the Communion question, as if it had been called to resolve it.[36]

Of course, synods surface strong disagreements and allow for hard questions to be asked. 'In an ecclesial context, stirring things up means

35 Pope Francis, Carta del Santo Padre al Cardenal Reinhard Marx, Arzobispo de Munchen und Freising, 10 June 2021 (my translation from the Spanish).
36 *Let Us Dream*, 87-88.

seeking the answers within synodality and not becoming a latter-day Savanarola who judges and condemns the Church,' notes the Superior General of the Society of Jesus, Fr Arturo Sosa, who adds: 'Disquieting questions need to be asked in order to kickstart discernment among other reasons, but they shouldn't lead to a parallel Church.'[37] Francis has constantly insisted that the synod is not a parliament called to debate and resolve a particular question, but a protected, privileged space for the ecclesial discernment of spirits prior to apostolic action in response. The Jesuits call this 'apostolic discernment in common': a process of searching for the will of God in which the apostolic group becomes the subject of the act of discernment. It is apostolic, in the sense that is geared towards service of the people, so that while there may be implications for church doctrine and practice, its purpose is pastoral and missionary. 'What is under discussion at synodal gatherings are not traditional truths of Christian doctrine. The Synod is concerned mainly with how teaching can be lived and applied in the changing contexts of our time,' notes Francis, who adds that the synods in his pontificate 'have played a vital role in opening up new ways of caring for people and places facing particular challenges'.[38]

Councils, assemblies and synods in the Catholic tradition are consultative rather than deliberative: decision-making power is reserved to the superior (the bishops, or in the case of the Synod of Bishops, the pope) who is assisted by the group in discerning. For there to be proper discernment, certain attitudes and actions are necessary, keeping in mind St Ignatius of Loyola's steps of an election process: seeking for true indifference (Sp, Exx #179), begging the light of the Holy Spirit (#180), weighing motives according to Gospel criteria, seeking confirmation of choice (#183), and testing spirits to unmask temptations, deceits (*sub angelo lucis*), and attachments.[39] This 'testing of the spirits' is especially important in a church context, where almost

37 Arturo Sosa SJ, *Walking with Ignatius: In conversation with Darío Menor* (2021, Chicago: Loyola Press), 83.

38 *Let Us Dream*, 85.

39 On discernment in common: Josep M. Rambla y Josep M. Lozano (eds.) *Discernimiento Comunitario Apostólico: Textos Fundamentales de la Compañía de Jesús* (Barcelona: Cristianisme i Justícia, October 2019).

everyone invokes the authority of 'tradition', 'the Gospel', 'Vatican II', 'God's will', 'true doctrine', and so on.

At the conclusion of all the synods, Francis has given an address in which he surveys the ways in which the Spirit had unmasked intentions. The 2015 gathering, for example, had been about 'laying bare closed hearts which frequently hide even behind the Church's teachings or good intentions, in order to sit in the chair of Moses and judge, sometimes with superiority and superficiality, difficult cases and wounded families'.[40] In the process of unmasking the Spirits, turbulence is not just normal but welcome. As Francis has said, 'the spiritual struggle, the movement of spirits, is a good sign ... to propose "something more" causes an agitation of the spirits when everything is suspiciously calm.'[41] Even the attempts to silence a synod or impose ideas on it, driven by panic and fear, are a 'good sign' because 'if the Spirit weren't present, those forces wouldn't bother'.[42]

In the family synods, and in the two that followed, Francis made a series of procedural changes to facilitate the pastoral, inductive approach, and to create space for the motions of the Spirit to be detected: less time for speeches to give more time for discussion in small groups; periods of silence to allow synod participants to sense motions of the spirits; reporting restrictions to help prevent journalists turning the synod into a contest between two sides, and other measures to facilitate the synod as a space for discernment rather than a parliamentary contest.

Yet it has not been easy. As long as the synod is regarded as a forum of competing notions of what is good and true — a place for debating ideas and persuading others of your view, rather than discerning the spirits — synodal discernment risks being sidetracked by traditionalists concerned with the defense of doctrine against perceived threats, or by progressives anxious to change the 'unjust' structures of the Church. One can see in Francis's interventions a certain exasperation. 'The Holy Spirit is the prime actor of the synod,' Francis pleaded

---

40 Pope Francis, 'Address at the conclusion of the Synod of Bishops', 24 October 2015.

41 Pope Francis, 'Miguel Angel Fiorito, Maestro di Dialogo', *La Civiltà Cattolica*, Quaderno 4070, 18 Gennaio 2020, 105-20.

42 *Let Us Dream*, 85.

at the start of the Amazonian synod. 'Please let us not drive him from the hall.' To the Church in Germany he stressed that 'synodality always presupposes and requires the irruption of the Holy Spirit'.

It has been hard to persuade progressives that the real question for the Pope after a synod is not whether this or that reform is good or what the Pope thinks but whether it is what the Spirit is asking of the Church at this time.[43] After the Central Committee of German Catholics (ZdK), an influential lay group which is jointly managing the Synodal Way with the German bishops' conference, accused Pope Francis of a 'lack of courage' for failing to move ahead on married priests and woman deacons, Francis told a US bishop: 'But the synod is not about the courage of the pope or the lack of the courage of the pope. The synod is about the action of the Holy Spirit and discernment of the Holy Spirit. And if there is no Holy Spirit, there is no discernment.'[44]

In *Let Us Dream* Francis spells out with clarity what it means to preside a synod with this responsibility, indeed, to govern the Church in deference to the Spirit. It implies, above all, humility: to be open to being possessed by the truth beyond our categories, rather than believing we are in possession of it; to renounce rigidity and uniformity: 'The Spirit always preserves the legitimate plurality of different groups and points of view, reconciling them in their diversity,' says Francis. A synod creates a new kind of harmony, in which what is good and valid on all sides is preserved in a new vision that transcends the parties in disagreement. It is hard work, requiring patience and commitment, holding in tension contrary views ('contrapositions') without allowing them to fall into contradiction and polarisation, and having an expectation of resolution 'by overflow' (*desborde*). In this way, the tensions in the body become not the cause of division but fruitful, leading to new ways of seeing, especially in a crisis:

43 See Ivereigh, 'Pope Francis: Reform & Resistance', *The Way*. Vol. 59, No. 4 (October 2020), 13-28.
44 '"A lack of courage": Germans divided over Pope Francis's Amazonian exhortation', Catholic News Agency, February 12, 2020. 'Pope shares with U.S. bishops his frustration with reaction to Amazon text', Catholic News Service. 13 February 2020.

At such moments, the solution to an intractable problem comes in ways that are unexpected and unforeseen, the result of a new and greater creativity released, as it were, from the outside. This is what I mean by "overflow" because it breaks the banks that confined our thinking, and causes to pour forth, as if from an overflowing fountain, the answers that formerly the contraposition didn't let us see. We recognize this process as a gift from God because it is the same action of the Spirit described in Scripture and evident in history … Such overflows of love happen, above all, at the crossroads of life, at moments of openness, fragility and humility, when the ocean of His love bursts the dams of our self-sufficiency, and so allows for a new imagination of the possible. [45]

Like a good spiritual director, Francis in *Let Us Dream* makes clear the attitudes synodality demands to keep us open to the Spirit's action while warning us against the temptations that close us off from it. One is to seek a false peace, an irenic avoidance of tension, a dishonest refusal to face the reality of conflict. Another is simplistic binary thinking that turns contrapositions into contradictions. In both cases, the Spirit is denied the freedom to act. In the case of the family synod, 'the Spirit saved us in the end': the breakthrough came in a new, properly Thomistic understanding of how the law should be applied in concrete circumstances. But in the Amazonian synod, while the 'overflow' was apparent in many areas, it did not appear in the celebrity issue of the ordination of married men, over which there was a deepening polarization. Without a sign of the breakthrough, Francis had no reason or right to introduce changes in that area, despite the narrow majority of bishops in favour. 'Sometimes walking together means continuing to endure the disagreements, leaving them to be transcended on a higher level at a later time,' he notes.[46]

Francis adds that his own interior discernment of the synod was 'confirmed by the discouragement that greeted the exhortation',

45 *Let Us Dream*, 80-81.
46 *Let Us Dream* 92. See also Austen Ivereigh, 'How to read "Querida Amazonia",
Commonweal magazine, 25 February 2020.

noting that within the synod process disappointment and a sense of defeat are not signs of the Good Spirit, for 'the Lord always keeps his promises'. Typically, disappointment reveals a pre-existing agenda: 'you come wanting to achieve something, and when you didn't get it, you feel deflated', a sign that 'you remain trapped within your desires, rather than allowing yourself to be touched by the grace on offer'.[47]

Francis's defense of discernment at the heart of synodality — the capacity to listen out for God's Spirit and to follow its direction — is inseparable from his understanding of the synod as an expression of the 'infallibility in believing' of the whole People of God. For Francis, the Spirit moves, above all, in the body of the people, acting to form the 'union of hearts and minds', a reconciled diversity that gives birth to fraternity. In *Episcopalis Communio* Francis says that 'the Synod of Bishops must increasingly become a privileged instrument for listening to the People of God. For the Synod Fathers we ask the Holy Spirit first of all for the gift of listening: to listen to God, that with him we may hear the cry of the people; to listen to the people until breathing in the desire to which God calls us'.

Fraternal dialogue is at the heart of synodality, allowing the Church to transcend the struggle between competing interests and worldviews. The 'first fruit of dialogue' is that 'each person opens up to novelty, to a change of opinion, to rejoice in what others say', he said at the synod on young people, while stressing the 'mystical fraternity' at the Amazonian synod.[48] What impedes fraternal dialogue is a distrustful self-withholding from the People of God that in *Let Us Dream* Francis describes as the 'isolated conscience'. The isolated conscience reflects a bad-spirit temptation to cling to one's own, narrow reasons — in defense of the 'acquired fortune' (the *cosa adquisita* of the *Spiritual Exercises*) — which over time harden into an elite ideology. 'Thus, are sown the seeds of division,' writes Francis. 'A charitable openness to the other is replaced by a clinging to the supposed superiority of one's own ideas.'[49]

---

47 *Let Us Dream*, 92.

48 Pope Francis, *Address at the beginning of the Synod dedicated to young people*, October 3, 2018, & *Greeting at the opening of the Special Assembly of the Synod of Bishops for the Pan-Amazonian Region*, 7 October 2019.

49 *Let Us Dream*, 72.

The alchemy of a synod open to the Spirit allows participants to enter into reciprocity with others and with God. It is a striking truth, Francis observes, that in Creation there is no contradiction: there is tension, contrast, diversity, but no contradiction. To fall into contradiction and polarisation is to withdraw from the reality of creation, into the lesser reality of our own ideas, to reject reciprocity in favour of the winter palaces of our own individual perceptions. Reality is discerned, says Francis, while ideas are debated. Parliaments debate ideas, synods demand discernment. To hear the Spirit in the assembly is to be healed of the illusion of my self-righteousness and self-enclosure. It is to make fraternity possible.

In *Let Us Dream* Francis offers three lessons from the 'ancient church experience of synodality' that can enable this fraternity. The first is the experience and practice of a respectful mutual listening in which the aim is not to reach agreement or win out in a contest of opposing positions but 'to journey together to seek God's will, allowing differences to harmonise' and to receive the 'new thing' that the Spirit wishes to offer. The second is to embrace that 'new thing', either as a breakthrough or overflow, or an invitation to change our thinking, shedding our rigidity and agendas, and opening us to new ways of seeing. The third is to accept the need for patience, to trust in processes of time: 'to pitch camp together, waiting for the skies to clear' (93-4).

A Church that embraces synodality in this way can be 'like a standard lifted up among the nations', Francis said in his 2015 speech, adding: 'let us cherish the dream that a rediscovery of the inviolable dignity of peoples and of the function of authority as service will also be able to help civil society to be built up in justice and fraternity.'[50] But for the Church to raise that standard, it must first embrace its own self: it must become synodal, to hear the Spirit in the Assembly. That remains the great task not just for Francis but, increasingly, for the whole Church in the twenty-first century.

---

50   Pope Francis, Address, Ceremony commemorating the 50th anniversary of the institution of the Synod of Bishops, 17 October 2015.

Questions

- *Ivereigh refers here to the 'genius' of Pope Francis. What particular words of Pope Francis highlighted in this article or in Let us Dream might the Irish Church focus on as it embarks on its synodal journey?*

- *What can the Irish church and others learn from the Aparecida process and experience as they prepare for and plan its own pathway towards synodality?*

3

ADVANCING THE RECEPTION OF THE COUNCIL. EPISCOPAL COLLEGIALITY, COLLEGIAL SYNODALITY, SYNODAL ECCLESIALITY

Rafael Luciani and Serena Noceti

Rafael Luciani is a Venezuelan lay theologian and a professor at the Catholic University in Caracas and Boston College's School of Theology and Ministry. Serena Noceti is an Italian lay theologian and a professor at the Religious Sciences Institute in Florence. In this chapter, they distinguish three related concepts: episcopal collegiality, collegial synodality and synodal ecclesiality. They outline the challenge involved in aligning these forms of synodality together and explore how the distinctive contributions of the magisterium, on the one hand, and of the laity, on the other, can and must be valued and integrated if synodality is to be authentic.

Professor Luciani is an expert advisor to CELAM (the Latin American Bishop's Council) and CLAR (the Latin American Confederation of Religious). Professor Nocetti is currently a member of the Ibero-American Theology Group for the Reform of the Church. Both Professors Luciani and Nocetti were advisers to the Ecclesial Network for the Pan-Amazonian Region during the Synod for the Pan-Amazonian Region (2019).

During the *Commemoration of the 50*th Anniversary of the Institution of the Synod of Bishops, Pope Francis called for a synodal Church. He said that 'it is precisely this path of synodality which God expects of the Church of the third millennium'[51]. Synodality is being proposed as a mode of being and acting that affects the Church's life, its instruments of discernment, and its structures of government. It is a constitutive dimension that qualifies ecclesiology, and defines a new way of proceeding that provides a form to the Church as People of God living in communion. While Vatican II proposed episcopal collegiality, Francis has moved this a step forward while proposing a collegial synodality. Deepening this path, the Latin American Church is giving birth to an ecclesial synodality. In this article we offer some key elements to understand the ecclesiological foundations of a Synodal Church.

'What is permanent is the people of God; what is transitory is the hierarchical service?'

During the Second Vatican Council many debates expressed the necessity of overcoming mentalities and structures that were inspired by the triumphalism, juridicism, and clericalism that had dominated the Church's life and mission for almost a millennium. The relations among ecclesial subjects — pope, bishops, clergy, laity — were viewed in the light of an unequal society. Bishop Émile-Joseph De Smedt explained it in these terms: 'You are familiar with the pyramid: pope, bishops, priests, each one of them responsible for teaching, sanctifying, and governing with their due authority. Then, at the base are the Christian people, who are mostly receptive, in a way that accords with the place they seem to occupy in the Church.' What was at issue was not a simple reversal of positions of power in the Church. De Smedt was very clear, affirming that 'what comes first is the People of God.' An ecclesiological shift was taking place, one that included all the faithful in the category of the People of God, granting them

<hr>

51 Francis. *Discourse at the Commemoration of 50th Anniversary of the Institution of the Synod of Bishops* (October 17, 2015) http://www.vatican.va/content/francesco/en/speeches/2015/october/documents/papa-francesco_20151017_50-anniversario-sinodo.html.

equal dignity and thus making them subjects with the same rights and duties as an ecclesial 'we'. Therefore, 'in the People of God we are all united with one another. We have the same basic laws and duties. We all share in the real priesthood of the people of God. The Pope is one of the faithful: bishops, priests, laity, religions, we are all the faithful'.[52]

This was a call for *a new way of proceeding*, one that included all ecclesial subjects as part of a *totality of the faithful*, opening a horizontal exercise of the *sensus fidelium* that integrates and qualifies the episcopal college and the successor of Peter into this totality of the people of God. This view had important implications. As Bishop De Smedt stated: 'It needs to be noted that hierarchical power is only transitory ... What is permanent is the people of God; what is temporary is the hierarchical service.' It´s interesting that in 1959 during the consultation with the Latin American Bishops to express their *vota* or proposals before the coming Council, Bishop Leonidas Proaño from Ecuador had already envisioned this ecclesiology of the People of God affirming that 'in the Church we are *all faithful*, baptized in Christ'.

In accord with the conciliar spirit, Pope Francis states that 'in this Church, as in an *inverted pyramid,* the peak is found below the base. That is why those who exercise authority are called "ministers": the original meaning of the word is "the smallest of all." Every bishop, by serving the People of God, becomes part of the flock that has been entrusted to him'[53]. The objective of inverting the pyramid is not to improve episcopal practice by seeking a better balance between papal primacy and the episcopal college, nor is it simply a redistribution of ecclesial co-responsibility. The real novelty consists in understanding the *People of God* as the *basic active and communal subject* of the whole Church and thus giving priority to evangelization — a responsibility of all — rather than to sacramentalization, which is reserved to the ministers, because the power of evangelizing, belonging to *all* is always superior to the power of baptizing, belonging to *some* (1 Cor 1:17).

In all of this, none of the faithful can be excluded from any ecclesial structure because the final objective and the *raison d'être* of any

52 Cf. *Acta Synodalia Sacrosancti Concilii Oecumenici Vaticani II*, 1/4, 142-143.
53 Francis, *Discourse at the Commemoration of 50th Anniversary of the Institution of the Synod of Bishops* (17 October 2015).

institutional structure of the Church is its *mission*, and the mission is determined and qualified by the participation of *all* in the *tria munera Christi* — priest, prophet and king — and not by the exercise of the ministerial authority resulting from ordination. Yet, this implies that a Synodal Church is only possible by *situating the hierarchy within the Ecclesiology of the People of God*, so that authority must be exercised within the framework of synodality.

'The renewal of the ecclesial hierarchy does not in itself produce transformation'

One of the necessary elements to implement Synodality today is the renewal of the hierarchy recognizing the inherent circularity that exists among the priesthood of the faithful and the ordained priesthood. Ordained ministry cannot exist nor be exercised in isolation without the other members of the faithful that form the People of God. In this perspective, one of the greatest advancements of the pontificate of Francis in regard to the reception of the Council has been aligning Chapters II and III of *Lumen Gentium* and proposing that both primacy and collegiality should be reformed by understanding their existence and exercise in function of the People of God.

We can understand this better if we situate ourselves within Chapter III of *Lumen Gentium*, recognizing that the unresolved juxtaposition between primacy and collegiality has given rise to a type of subordinate relationship that has not helped synodal reform. Even the notion of 'college' did not have an easy time making its way through the Council. Countering the pressure of the conservative minority, who wanted to save the doctrine of primacy promulgated by Vatican I, Paul VI added an explanatory note to *Lumen Gentium*, making it clear that:

> the Supreme Pontiff, as Supreme Pastor of the Church, may freely exercise his power at any time, as his own ministry requires of him. In contrast, the College, although it always exists, does not for that reason act permanently with *strictly* collegial action. … It acts with strictly collegial action only at intervals and *with the consent of the Head* (*LG. Nota Praevia* 4).

This created an unresolved juxtaposition (*LG* 22) between Chapters II [People of God] and III [Hierarchy] of *Lumen Gentium*, and led to a concentration of power and authority in the hierarchy by reason of ordination, thus provoking a difficulty in understanding synodality not only in terms of more participative relations among ecclesial subjects, but also in terms of the structural reform of the institutions.

Trying to solve this, the International Theological Commission in its document on *Synodality in the life and mission of the Church* recovers the hermeneutical key to reading the Council's ecclesiology:

> the sequence [of *Lumen Gentium*] — Mystery of the Church (Chapter I), People of God (Chapter II), Hierarchical Constitution of the Church (Chapter III) — makes it clear that the *ecclesiastical hierarchy is placed at the service of the People of God* so that the mission of the Church is carried out in conformity with the divine design of salvation, following the logic that gives priority to the whole over the parts and to the end over the means.[54]

Therefore, while collegiality refers to the nature and form proper to the episcopacy as it is exercised among bishops with and under Peter (*LG* 22-23), synodality is instead *a constitutive mark of the whole ecclesial life and its form*; it is *the whole Church's way of proceeding*, and, therefore, it involves the totality of the People of God joined together by means of reciprocal identities. This being the case, collegiality must be conceived and understood on the basis of synodality, and not vice versa. Therefore, synodality 'offers us the most adequate interpretative framework for understanding the hierarchical ministry itself'.[55]

Here we find the authentic ecclesiological shift of the Council received and advanced by Francis's pontificate: what we call the *principle*

---

54 International Theological Commission, *Synodality in the life and mission of the Church* (2 March 2018) http://www.vatican.va/roman_curia/congregations/cfaith/cti_documents/rc_cti_20180302_sinodalita_sp.html.

55 International Theological Commission, *Synodality in the life and mission of the Church* (2 March 2018).

of the totality of the faithful. The institutionalization of this principle is what will allow the Church to move beyond the clericalization of ecclesial culture, the sacerdotalization of ministries and the lack of accountability. The words Francis addressed to the Chilean bishops are instructive: 'the Church's immune system resides in that *faithful* and silent people' (Private Letter to the Bishops of Chile). But assuming the centrality of the ecclesiology of the People of God in the Council and recognizing synodality as a new *mark* of the Church, brings new meaning and powerful implications to this word: *faithful.*

The people of God as the totality of the faithful

While it is true that the Church builds up communion to the extent that it becomes constituted as the People of God (*EG* 113), it cannot achieve this goal except through a *synodal form* and a *synodal way of proceeding.*[56] This means giving primacy to the ecclesial form of knowing called *sensus fidei,* which is a capacity given to every baptized person, but only when exercised as *sensus fidelium,* that is, as part of the totality of baptized persons. This is what Vatican II teaches when it states that:

> The *entire body of the faithful,* anointed as they are by the Holy One (cf. 1 John 2.20, 27), cannot err in matters of belief. They manifest this special property by means of the whole people's supernatural discernment in matters of faith when "from the Bishops down to the last of the lay faithful" they show universal agreement in matters of faith and morals (*LG* 12).

The ecclesiological shift of the Council has to do with the notion of the *totality of the faithful,* or all the faithful understood within a logic of reciprocity. In *Evangelii Gaudium* (*EG* 119, 198), we find further this development of the teaching of *Lumen Gentium* (*LG* 9 and 12), with the use of the notion of *sensus fidei,* when speaking of the whole People of God as called to discipleship and mission. The faithful are

---

56 Cf. Rafael Luciani, 'Reforma, conversión pastoral y sinodalidad. Un nuevo modo eclesial de proceder'. Rafael Luciani (ed.). *La sinodalidad en la vida de la Iglesia. Reflexiones para contribuir a la reforma eclesial,* San Pablo, Madrid 2020, 41-66.

not understood as a collection of individuals or as an undifferentiated mass; rather, they are understood as a *body* joined in the *reciprocal interaction* that arises from the participation of each member *suo modo et pro sua parte* (*LG* 31) in the mission of the Church in the world by way of discipleship. From this point of view, we can then speak of the novelty of synodality.

According to this vision, we can say that the *sensus fidelium* and the *magisterium* are distinct but *complementary* subjects whose constant reciprocity produces and regulates the intelligence of faith. If this were not so, the deposit of faith (*depositum fidei*) would become an abstract, unilateral reality without any connection to the People of God. The unity between these two subjects does not result from the similarity in the way they exercise that function, but in the necessity of interrelating both subjects in order to achieve an authentic *sensus fidei ecclesiae*, that should express itself in a mandatory *ecclesial consensus*. If the two subjects are complementary, the *consensus omnium fidelium* should be the fruit of a *sensus fidei totius populi* because all ecclesial subjects are called to interact. Here, it is proper to the task of the bishops, as guarantors of the Apostolicity of the faith and custodians of the *Ecclesial We*, to promote and guide everyone to the *consensus fidelium*. Therefore, in a synodal Church, the elaboration of a *consensus* among all ecclesial subjectivities depends on the discernment of the whole, and not of the Bishops (the *many*) or the Pope (the *one*), since discernment is not only done in the Church, but it *makes the Church* insofar it should be a true expression of the *sensus ecclesiae* and not of the Bishops.

According to Francis, some processes stand out. First, the 'listening of all the faithful', and not only of the Bishops or the Episcopal Conferences. Second, 'processes of community discernment' in two phases: by local or regional assemblies that are convoked prior to the Synodal Assembly, leading to a *Working Document* that is not prepared nor imposed by the Curia; and by the Synodal Assembly with the participation of those who vote and those who do not vote. And third, the interpretation proper to the episcopal college assembled together leads to a 'final decision' made by the Pope. Decisions are made after discerning what the assembly of Bishops voted for and expressed in the *Final Document* of the Synod. Throughout this process all members of the People of God achieve and 'constitute a singular consensus of all the faithful' (*Dei verbum* 10). This form and way of proceeding can be appreciated in the way in which Francis has advanced in the understanding and realization of his different Synods that led to a reform in *Episcopalis Communio* in 2018. But let us remember that synodality is more than a Synod, because it's a new *mark* of the whole Church. Not distinguishing this, limits the understanding of the novelty and the ecclesiological implications of synodality in regard to the reform of the Church mentalities and structures.

The elaboration and the making of decisions in the construction of consensus

Pope Francis follows Paul VI's teaching in *Apostolica sollicitudo*, then assumed in *Christus Dominus* 5, considering the Synod of Bishops as an instrument at the service of the exercise of Papal primacy. But, on the other hand, the Pope broadens the perspective and relocates the service of the college of Bishops and the Pope on the horizon of an entirely Synodal Church. We can hold that, throughout the Synods, Francis has advanced from *episcopal collegiality*, proper to the Second Vatican Council, to *collegial synodality*, proper to the ecclesiology of this pontificate. The form and the way of proceeding of the Synods that the Pope has convoked can be considered as an emergence of a *collegial synodality*. As Francis explains: 'Although structurally it is essentially configured as an episcopal body, this does not mean that the Synod exists separately from the rest of the faithful. On the contrary, it is a suitable instrument to *give voice to the entire People of God*' (*Episcopalis Communio*, 6).

The reform of a structure like that of the Synod cannot be seen only as a matter of *method*; such a reform has already been achieved in the recent synodal assemblies convoked by Francis. A more thorough reform of this institution or the creation of another one needs to be seen in the relationship between *collegial synodality* and *synodal ecclesiality*, which is evidently expressed in the processes of discerning and elaborating decisions in order to build an ecclesial consensus. This means considering the forms of interaction among the different ecclesial subjects during all stages of the processes that lead to a final decision.

An initial approach to this perspective can be recognized in the former Synod for the Amazon that started out from the lowest point possible so that the *process for elaborating decisions* began with the whole People of God and not with a pre-elaborated document. A next step should need to think how the *subsequent process*, which corresponds to the one (Pope) or the many (Bishops) who make the decisions, can *ratify what was elaborated by all* (the faithful). This will truly express the fruit of an interaction of the totality of the faithful, from below and from within, so that the consultative organs *elaborate* the decision which the pastoral authority then *assumes*, because they all participate as faithful in the whole process.

Although the Code of Canon Law gives the Pontiff the ability to concede a deliberative and binding force to the decision of the bishops (Canon 343), the episcopal institution continues to be a body of collaboration and counsel that expresses only affective collegiality (*Christus Dominus* 5). In order for this to change and become effective, the Pope would have to *ratify and promulgate* the conclusion reached by the synodal fathers, as we have said. However, even here we see a development that allows the practice of *episcopal collegiality* as *collegial synodality*, when Francis opens the possibility — in Article 18 of *Episcopalis Communio* — to ratify and promulgate the *Final Document* of a Synod making it part of his ordinary Magisterium as Successor of Peter. In an initial way, this appears in *Querida Amazonia*, the Post-Synodal Exhortation of the Pan-Amazonian Synod, where the Pope clearly states that the Post-Synodal Exhortation does not substitute for the *Final Document of the Synod* (*QA* 2), but rather *assumes* it (*QA* 3) inviting people to read it integrally (*QA* 3) and *apply* it (*QA* 4). This represents a recovery, though yet to be realized, of a Local Churches' ecclesiology.

The emergence of a *synodal ecclesiality: new paths from the peripheries*

Currently, the Church in Latin American is giving birth to what we have called *synodal ecclesiality*. This has initially happened in *Medellín*[57] — the Second General Conference of the Latin American Bishops — and at the *Venezuelan Plenary Council*.[58] But more recently this way of proceeding has been reassumed with great novelty in the process of re-structuring of the *Latin American Bishops Council* (CELAM) and the creation of the *Ecclesial Conference of the Amazon* (CEAMA). It's important here to emphasize that it's not an *Episcopal* but an *Ecclesial Conference*.

A *synodal ecclesiality* is the fruit of a co-shared vision and exercise of governance, and the binding nature of the decision-making and decision-taking processes where all *people* participate, "from Bishops to the last of the lay faithful" (*Episcopalis Communio* 5). This ecclesial *way of proceeding* can be found, as an emerging element, in what *Aparecida* — the Fifth General Conference of the Latin American Bishops — mandated in 2007 and inspires Francis: 'the laity should participate in *the discernment, the decision making, the planning,* and *the execution*' (*Aparecida* 371). But in order for *synodal ecclesiality* to work, it is essential to relate the Synod of Bishops to listening processes within local churches. As an example, local diocesan synods or ecclesial assemblies can be convoked in advance of the Synod of Bishops. This will contribute, from bottom to top, to the listening of the faithful in each local church. But it also needs to develop and give form to deliberative processes in a more complex form, including, for example, discernment of realities on the ground, evaluation of options, valuing the ways in which decisions are taken, and following up the implementation and the evaluation processes.[59]

---

57 Cf. Rafael Luciani, 'From Collegiality to Synodality in Latin America', *Asian Horizons: Dharmaram Journal of Theology* 14 (2020) 151-166.

58 Cf. Raúl Biord Castillo, 'El Concilio Plenario de Venezuela. Una buena experiencia sinodal (2000-2006)', in Rafael Luciani (ed.), *La sinodalidad en la vida de la Iglesia. Reflexiones para contribuir a la reforma eclesial*, San Pablo, Madrid 2020, 293-328.

59 Cf. Serena Noceti, 'Elaborare decisioni nella chiesa. Una riflessione ecclesiologica', in R. Battocchio – L. Tonello (edd.), *Sinodalità. Dimensione della Chiesa, pratiche nella chiesa*. EMP, Padova 2020, 237-254.

Open conclusion

As seen throughout this brief reflection, synodality expresses an ecclesial *form* and a *new way of proceeding* that 'has its point of departure but also its point of arrival in the *People of God*' (*Episcopalis Communio* 7). The challenge is to maintain the specific contribution of the episcopal and papal magisterium and the equally specific and unique contribution of laity, men and women, who offer charisms, cultures and the specificity of gender, at all levels in the Church. New steps are needed or we will continue to have an insufficient theological and pastoral appreciation of the *sensus fidelium,* an isolated exercise of authority and a centralized style of governance in the Church. We can conclude saying that 'in the synodal Church the whole community, in the free and rich diversity of its members, is called together to pray, listen, analyse, dialogue, discern and offer advice on taking pastoral decisions'.[60]

Questions:

- Church structure is described here as a pyramid, a form we are all familiar with in Church governance. If an ecclesiological shift, like that desired by Pope Francis is to happen as a result of the universal synod, what shape will a post-synodal Church take on?

- Clericalism and hierarchicalism are both identified here as having contributed to the current structure and way of being in our Church. How do they fit with the notion of a synodal Church which truly represents the totality of the faithful?

---

60   International Theological Commission, *Synodality in the life and mission of the Church* (2 March 2018).

4

SYNODALITY: TOWARD A RENEWAL OF MINISTRY

Responding to Clericalism and the Call for Sharing Ministry in the Church

Nathalie Becquart, xmcj

Nathalie Becquart is a member of the Xaverian Missionaries of Christ Jesus (xmcj) and Under-Secretary at the Holy See's General Secretariat of the Synod of Bishops. In this chapter she puts forward a vision for ministry in a synodal Church. Realising this vision will mean ridding the Church of the scourge of clericalism and replacing it with a servant leader model of Church both in theory and in practice.

Sr Becquart previously directed the National Service for the Evangelization of Young People and for Vocations for the French Bishops' Conference and has undertaken postgraduate studies at Boston College's School of Theology and Ministry with a focus on ecclesiology.

The shock resignation of Pope Benedict XVI and the shift in pastoral leadership exemplified by Pope Francis are just two examples of the Church confronting various issues around power, theology, and renewal in the twenty-first century. Central to the corruption of power and the tragedy of the abuse crisis is the scourge of clericalism. 'Clericalism, whether fostered by priests themselves or by lay persons, leads to an excision in the ecclesial body that supports and helps to perpetuate many of the evils that we are condemning today. To say "no" to abuse is to say an emphatic "no" to all forms of clericalism.'[61] Clericalism can only be addressed by the whole People of God by which power is shared by all, baptised and ordained, in the service of all.[62]

Although Pope Francis's diagnosis of clericalism is shared by many,[63] the concrete solutions are yet to be sketched out or discerned.[64] One major aspect of this 'systemic' multifaceted reality of clericalism is the

---

61 "If one member suffers, all suffer together with it" (1 Cor 12:26). These words of Saint Paul forcefully echo in my heart as I acknowledge once more the suffering endured by many minors due to sexual abuse, the abuse of power and the abuse of conscience perpetrated by a significant number of clerics and consecrated persons" Francis, *Letter to the People of God*, 20 August 2018.

62 This diagnosis of clericalism that Pope Francis never cease to denounced is highlighted by many theologians and church leaders but has also been stated by independent national commissions on sexual abuses such as the Royal Commission in Australia Australia - Royal Commission into Institutional Responses to Child Sexual Abuse, et Peter McClellan, *Final Report* (Sydney, N.S.W.: Royal Commission into Institutional Responses to Child Sexual Abuse, 2017), https://www.childabuseroyalcommission. gov.au/final-report.and the MHG-Studie in Germany – *Forschungsprojekt, Sexueller Missbrauch an Minderjährigen durch katholische Priester, Diakone und männliche Ordensangehörige im Bereich der Deutschen Bischofskonferenz* https://www.dbk.de/file-admin/redaktion/diverse_downloads/dossiers_2018/MHG-Studie-gesamt.pdf

63 'Clericalism, whether fostered by priests themselves or by lay persons, leads to an excision in the ecclesial body that supports and helps to perpetuate many of the evils that we are condemning today.' Francis, *Letter to the People of God*, 20 August 2018.

64 'Change in direction, the step that must follow the admission of failure if the future is to be different from the past, may be no less arduous than its predecessor. Effective replacements for flawed strategies do not materialize as if by magic, nor are they regularly identical with the first available option, especially if that option is plundered feverishly. Rather, the development of policies and practices that serve the well-being of communities and individuals requires creativity and imagination, time and patience, efforts to build reliable coalitions, and a willingness to grapple with questions that defy simple answers.' Richard Lennan,'Beyond Scandal and Shame? Ecclesiology and the Longing for a Transformed Church', *Theological Studies* 2019, Vol. 80(3), 590–610.

exercise of power.[65] To overcome clericalism we must reflect deeply on the question of power and ministry in the Church[66] so as to create a culture of authentic Christian authority.[67] Understood according to the theological perspective defined by Richard Gaillardetz in his book *By what authority?:*

> For our purposes, we may think of "power" simply as the capacity for effective action and ecclesial power, when it is exercised authentically, as the capacity to engage in effective action in service of the Church's life and mission. "Authority," in turn, can be understood as the legitimate, trustworthy, and accountable exercise of power.[68]

In this essay I shall explore synodality as a response of the Church in the third millennium to a renewal of ecclesiology and pastoral practice, towards an inclusive leadership overcoming clericalism and recognizing the shared responsibility of all the baptized. To understand the importance of synodality as central to this response, I first look at ecclesiology from an historical and theological perspective. Secondly, I address the notion of power and authority in relation to ministry and service in the Church. Finally, I suggest some theological and pastoral ways to envision the notion of power in ministry as 'a generative force

---

65 As already proposed by Yves Congar, *Pour une Eglise servante et pauvre: le livre-programme du pape François* (Paris: Cerf, 2014), 140.

66 Richard R. Gaillardetz, *By What Authority?: Foundations for Understanding Authority in the Church*, Revised and expanded edition.. (Collegeville, Minn.: Liturgical Press, 2018).

67 "The "never again" to the culture of abuse and the system of cover up that allows it to be perpetuated demands working among everyone in order to generate a culture of care which permeates our ways of relating, praying, thinking, of living authority; our customs and languages and our relationship with power and money" Francis, *Letter to the Church of Chile*, 5 June 2018.

68 And he adds: 'Note also that you can have power without authority, but you can't have authority without power,' which implies that 'Christians should not yield so easily to this narrow, dominating understanding of power. In truth, any form of authentic human existence will require the exercise of power in relation to others, and this is no less true within the church'.

... to liberate the freedom'.[69] That means a practice of power within a synodal Church is an on-going process of discernment exercised from a pattern of servant leadership and collegiality. This requires teamwork and accountability, reflection and supervision, initial and ongoing formation, so as to form ministers – baptized and ordained – who work together in the spirit of synodality.

Part I – Where do we come from? Where are we?

In 1963, Yves Congar reflected: 'A great deal still remains to be done to declericalize our conception of the Church, and to put the clergy back where they truly belong in the place of member-servants'.[70] In contrast with the ecclesiological framework set up by Vatican II that highlights the equal dignity of all the baptized, we are still influenced by our long history of ministry since the Middle Ages, marked by a stark distinction between ordained clergy and non-ordained laity.

New Testament presents a range of ministers in the Church but this situation has been transformed through a process of institutionalization that concentrated ministry principally on the figure of the ordained. This phenomenon of the sacerdotalization of ministry has given rise to a priestly class centred on the Eucharist, shaped on one side by the exercise of power in the Constantinian Empire and then, on the other side, by the hierarchical organization of the society in the Middle Ages.

With Thomas Aquinas, the idea of a special permanent character imprinted at ordination perpetuated a high theology of ordained priesthood. Trent, in reaction to the Reformation,[71] emphasized the link between the priesthood and Eucharist in such a way that distanced the clergy theologically from the lay faithful. The 'hierarchical' model of Church described as 'a pyramidal, perfect society'

---

69 According to the expressions in of the Final Document of the Synod of Bishops on Young People, Faith and Vocational Discernment §71 http://www.synod2018.va/content/synod2018/en/fede-discernimento-vocazione/final-document-of-the-synod-of-bishops-on-young-people--faith-an.html

70 Yves Congar, *Pour une Église Servante et Pauvre* (Paris: Les Éditions du Cerf, 1963), 113.

71 *Après Trente réaction Réforme*, 'd'un côté, elle a réaffirmé l'autorité et l'a davantage concentrée; de l'autre côté, elle en a révisé la conception et la pratique au plan moral et pastoral', ibid., 56.

turned to be a 'hierarchology', according to Yves Congar, creating an imbalanced relationship between *ecclesia docens* and *ecclesia discens*, the governors and the governed, the cleric and the lay.[72] It generates pastoral relationships that are 'fundamentally marked by the inequality of power. This hierarchical stratification creates enormous potential to take advantage of the vulnerability of those seeking pastoral advice'.[73]

Thus, today, we are in a complex landscape shaped by inner tensions along conflictual models of ministry and ecclesiology. The post-Vatican II vision of ordained priesthood is drawn through a broad and dynamic approach within a pattern that could be characterized by a move from a functional, ontological, 'monarchical' understanding of what was called sacerdotal ministry (*sacerdos*) to a sacramental, relational and spiritual understanding of what is now named presbyteral ministry (*presbyteros*). This vision places the authority and exercise of power of ordained ministers within the matrix of service.

The complexity of the current background of the topic of power in the Church has to be understood in the light of a double internal and external influence. Internally, is the emergence of lay ecclesial ministers in many countries like the US and France challenging the 'ministerial system' of the Church after Vatican II redistributing the exercise of authority and ministry? Externally, the Church is not immune to the enormous paradigmatic institutional shifts in society since 1968 changing the shape and exercise of authority.

Our societies have become societies of communication that shake up previous patterns of transmission and exercise of power. We can sum it up with this popularized formula: 'the tyranny of peers has replaced the tyranny of fathers'. Western liberal democracies are traversed by two opposite movements. One movement is particularly

---

72 Richard Gula, *Just Ministry: Professional Ethics for Pastoral Ministers* (Mahwah, NJ: Paulist, 2010), 118.
73 Ibid., 119.

visible among young people who have a culture of participation[74] and are operating more and more horizontally: they distrust institutions; they ask to be protagonists and co-actors of organizations and groups they belong to. The other movement is probably developed in reaction to this shift from a vertical to a horizontal structure. It favors authoritarian power and is revealed by the rise of populism. In fact, the challenge in deciphering the current situation is undoubtedly to hold together trends that are antagonistic to each other while at the same time finding a way to govern that allows for opposing positions. I suggest thinking and figuring out the social and ecclesial dynamics at work by using the literary figure of the oxymoron. In this context, servant leadership aiming to serve all the community in its diversity implies an inherent internal tension in the context of today characterized as it is by fragmentation and polarisation. The figure of the oxymoron can help to understand and work out a possible creative path of a style of leadership not afraid to cope with tensions.

Thus, the question of the exercise of power in ministry today has to be understood in the context of the immense change of relationships towards authority and power in the society. The question of power in the Church at this time of the sexual abuses crisis has to be considered within this socio-cultural and political landscape of our societies both marked by a patriarchal heritage, which shapes many relationships in a structure of inequality and, at the same time, by a greater and greater aspiration and implementation of true relationships of equality and parity. The recent phenomenon of the #MeToo movement reveals the extent of the abuses of power in so many areas, beginning with families but also largely present in different fields like education, sport, cinema, politics and business. We have to situate the question

---

74 Final Document of the synod of bishops on young people, *The young want active involvement*: 'In the face of society's contradictions, many young people wish to offer the fruits of their talents, skills and creativity and they are ready to assume responsibility. Among the themes they hold most dear are social and environmental sustainability, discrimination and racism. The involvement of the young often follows entirely new paths, and this includes harnessing the potential of digital communication in terms of mobilization and political pressure: spread of lifestyles and critical models of consumption and investment, in solidarity and attentive to the environment; new forms of commitment and participation in society and in politics; new forms of welfare in aid of the weakest', 52.

of power in the Church within this contemporary context,[75] as ministers are human persons from their time. But at once we have to identify and take into account that the specificity of the ecclesial conception and practice of power exercised by ordained ministers is structurally viewed as a sacred power coming from God.[76]

Thus, we have to acknowledge that the practice of power in ministry in the Catholic Church is relying not only on human factors linked to the personality of ministers, but also on a theology of power intertwined with a medieval theology of priesthood coming from an ontological vision. It is not only a question of mentality, culture and individual failures, but the tragedy of an institutional failure that requires re-interrogating the structures and also requires a Reform of the Church[77] and an important rethinking of our theology.

Pope Francis reminds us that the renewal of leadership and the eradication of clericalism necessitate the cooperation of the whole Body of Christ. '[T]he renewal of the Church hierarchy by itself does not create the transformation to which the Holy Spirit moves us. We are required together to promote a transformation of the Church that involves us all'.[78]

> [Thus] the "never again" to the culture of abuse and the system of cover up that allows it to be perpetuated demands working with everyone in order to generate a culture of care that permeates our ways of relating, praying, thinking, of living authority; our customs and languages and our relationship with power and money.[79]

75 'The abuse crisis in the Catholic Church cannot be separated from other crises, for example, the "MeToo" movement, and the anti-institutionalism that affects all institutions.' Massimo Faggioli, 'The Catholic Sexual Abuse Crisis as a Theological Crisis: Emerging Issues,' *Theological Studies* (2019), Vol. 80 (3), 573.
76 'Le gouvernement est, dans l'Eglise, un pouvoir reçu de Dieu, mais possédé d'une manière telle que l'Eglise l'exerce pleinement par elle-même et *positis ponendis*, comme une autorité politique peut exercer son propre pouvoir de gouvernement,' Yves Congar, *Vraie et fausse réforme dans l'Eglise*, (Paris: Editions du Cerf, 1950), 111.
77 Cf Carlos Schickendantz, 'Fracaso institucional de un modelo teológico-cultural de Iglesia Factores sistémicos en la crisis de los abusos', *Teologia y vida* 60 (2019), no. 1, 9-39.
78 Francis, *Letter to the Church of Chile, June 5, 2018, 1*.
79 Ibid., 4.

We can identify three key factors in the fraught relationship between clerical power and the abuse crisis. The first factor, observed by Alphonse Borras in his works on synodality, is the overly personal manner in which power is exercised in the Latin Church.[80] The second factor that makes possible the first is the fact that, in the Catholic Church, ministers can exercise their power without accountability.[81] Thirdly, these two factors impede true listening to the *sensus fidelium*[82] and the commitment to victims over and above the reputation of the institution. All of this calls for a serious reflection on the abuse of power so as to renew ministry in the Church.[83] By valuing victims over institutions, the Church must move down a path of healing from its deep wounds. This implies a death to an idealized form of the Church to a rebirth and rise of another form.[84]

---

80 « L'Eglise catholique latine est marquée depuis de longs siècles par l'exercice personnel de l'autorité pastorale, au détriment de l'exercice collégial sensus lato c'est-à-dire en référence à « quelques-uns », et de l'exercice communautaire impliquant plus largement la communauté, à savoir dans la référence à « tous », l'ensemble des baptisés comme corps ecclésial du Christ » Alphonse BORRAS, *Communion ecclésiale et synodalité*, CLD 2019, . 113

81 'Le fait que, dans l'Église catholique, le pouvoir hiérarchique s'exerce classiquement sans que ses détenteurs aient de comptes à rendre, constitue un troisième paramètre.' Hervé LeGrand, 'Abus sexuels et cléricalisme'. *Etudes* no. 4259 (2019), 90.

82 Enfin, un quatrième paramètre explicatif réside dans un magistère hiérarchique peu à l'écoute du *sensus fidelium* (sens de la foi de l'ensemble des fidèles) et réticent à promouvoir la réflexion permanent dans l'Église. Ibid., 91.

83 'There may be unanimity about the need for change, but a program for positive change, as well as the means to accomplish it, has not yet reached the same degree of agreement across the Catholic community. At least in part, this lack of consensus results from the large number of issues where change in the church seems to be not merely desirable, but long overdue. From lay participation in ecclesial governance to practices of formation for ordained ministry, and from the leadership of women to the church's learning from a socially and religiously pluralistic world, Catholics longing for a more transparent and accountable church have multiple options to canvas.' Richard Lennan, 'Beyond Scandal and Shame? Ecclesiology and the Longing for a Transformed Church', *Theological Studies* 80:3 (2019), 592.

84 'A solid grasp of the dignity of the baptized is, in fact, essential to reform. It grounds both laity and clergy. But getting to the point where this is truly grasped involves more than a cosmetic change. It actually entails dying to one vision of church and rising to another.' Rita Ferrone 'The abuse crisis as prophecy and pascha', *Commonweal*, 12 April 2019.

Part II – Towards a vision of power in ministry as servant leadership within a synodal church

The sexual abuse scandal has deeply shaken the Church. This is not least because it has also occurred in the context of post-modernity, which of itself has brought about considerable 'fluidity' and 'uncertainty' across society[85] and led to serious questions being asked about the validity of all institutions. This time of crisis is a call to change and to re-envision the Church, to open new paths for the proclamation of the Gospel in the world of today. It is an opportunity[86] to embrace a necessary path of reform which so many people, especially women and young people, are longing for.[87]

The new ways to build one's identity and the new processes of socialization based on subjectivity and personal choices overturn established powers and traditional vertical systems of authority.[88] Sociologists say that formerly people built their identity through clear inherited belongings and commitments.[89] Now we have gone from a paradigm of belonging, to a paradigm of experimentation. That means people's self-identity is no longer shaped by predetermined collective belonging but by a chosen belonging they need to experience. The institutional failure revealed by the abuse crisis and cover-up coupled

85   Marked by 'radical cultural diversity and irreducible pluralism.' Serena Noceti, 'Church, a Living Community. The Challenge of Fragility', *Journal of the European Society of Women in Theological Research* 16 (2008), 138.

86   'The Lord Jesus, who never abandons his Church, offers her the strength and the tools to set out on a new path. Confirming the line of timely "actions and sanctions that are so necessary" (Francis, *Letter to the People of God, 20 August 2018, 2*) and aware that mercy demands justice, the Synod recognizes that confronting the question of abuse in all its aspects, not without the valuable help of the young, can truly be an opportunity for a reform of epoch-making significance', *Final Document of the Synod on Young People, 31.*

87   'Today's young people are longing for an authentic Church. We want to say, especially to the hierarchy of the Church, that they should be a transparent, welcoming, honest, inviting, communicative, accessible, joyful and interactive community', *Final Document of the pre-synod*, 11.

88   Nathalie Becquart, 'L'Esprit renouvelle tout. Une pastorale des jeunes avec les jeunes', *Salvator* (2020), 63.

89   For instance the works of Pr. Jean-Marie Donegani in France, in La sécularisation du croire, *Archives de sciences sociales des religions* (2015) no. 169, or in 'Individu, sujet, communauté' in *Eglise et vocations*, no. 2 (May 2008).

with the end of the 'system-era' compels the Church to rediscover its own fragility and re-examine its structures, process and methods of exercising power to better fulfill her mission.

Pope Francis's call to embrace the path of synodality as the call of God for the Church of the third millennium[90] gives us both a renewed vision for leadership and an antidote to clericalism. Pope Francis's vision of synodality as 'constitutive of the Church' is rooted in a re-evaluation of the Council's theology of the People of God (especially *Lumen Gentium*, Chapter 2) and the influence of the Argentinian theology of the People that shaped his ministry as a Jesuit and archbishop of Buenos Aires. This theology emphasizes the *sensus fidei*[91] and the equal dignity of all the baptized called to be missionary disciple.[92]

In the vision of Pope Francis, synodality is linked with the pastoral conversion of the Church inspired by the CELAM conference of Santo Domingo. 'The notion of pastoral conversion is proposed as an organic and structural axis of the whole genesis and ecclesial organization, affecting "everything and everyone" in relationship to lifestyles (personal and community praxis), exercises of authority and power (relationships of equality and authority), and ecclesial models (structures and dynamisms).'[93] The two key elements of the People of God/*sensus fidelium* and pastoral conversion are central to ending

---

90 'The world in which we live, and which we are called to love and serve, even with its contradictions, demands that the Church strengthen cooperation in all areas of her mission. It is precisely this path of *synodality which God expects of the Church of the third millennium.*' Francis, address for the ceremony commemorating the 50th anniversary of the institution of the synod of bishops, 17 October 2015.

91 '[Christ] fulfils this prophetic office, not only through the hierarchy who teach in his name and by his power but also through the laity. He accordingly both establishes them as witnesses and provides them with an appreciation of the faith (sensus fidei) and the grace of the word so that the power of the Gospel may shine out in daily family and social life', *Lumen Gentium*, 35.

92 'The focus on synodality echoes the renewed interest in the *sensus fidei* of all the baptized, and in the necessity for the *sensus fidelium* of the whole church to be understood as radically other than the passive obedience of one section of the church's membership to another. These emphases witness to the conviction that "the church listens to the Spirit when all listen to one another". I cannot find where this has come from.'

93 Rafael Luciani, 'Reforma, conversion pastoral y sinodalidad. Un nuevo modo eclesial de proceder, Maria Teresa Compte and Rafael Luciani (eds.), *En camino hacia una Iglesia Sinodal: de Pablo VI a Francisco*, (PPC, Madrid, 2020), 170.

clericalism, which involves not only the ordained but all of the baptized. 'It is impossible to think of a conversion of our activity as a Church that does not include the active participation of all the members of God's People.'[94]

At the heart of synodality is listening:

> A synodal Church is a Church of listening, with the awareness that listening "is more than hearing" (12). It is a mutual listening in which everyone has something to learn. The faithful people, the Episcopal College, the Bishop of Rome, each one listening to others; and all listening to the Holy Spirit, the "Spirit of Truth" (Jn 14:17), to know what he says to the Churches (Rev 2:7).[95]

This dynamic vision of synodality presents the Church in its historical dimension in a state of permanent birth, in an on-going process of reform. It lets us perceive that the identity of the Church is a dynamic identity, not a static one; it is a relational identity of communion-mission rooted in the Trinitarian mystery and the Eucharistic mystery. This identity of the Church manifested through the concept of synodality tells us that it is a Church in movement, a Church in emergence (in connection with the concept of ecclesiogenesis or ecclesiogenetics). A synodal church is a relational church where all the People of God, where their vocation and position, are in interdependence and mutuality. The minister doesn't exist outside the community. He is not separate from the people to whom he ministers.[96] 'Ministry doesn't exist as a power or reality in its own right but only as linked to pastoral service.'[97]

---

94 Francis, *Letter to the Church of Chile*, June 5, 2018.

95 Ibid.

96 'There is to be no distance or separation between the community and its Pastors – who are called to act in the name of the only Pastor – but a distinction between tasks in the reciprocity of communion.' Ibid., 69.

97 Richard Gaillardetz, 'The Ecclesiological Foundations of Ministry within an Ordered Communion', in Susan Wood, ed., *Ordering the Baptismal Priesthood: Theologies of Lay and Ordained Ministry*, (Collegeville, MN: Liturgical Press, 2003), 38.

Thus, decisions have to be taken through synodal processes that require listening to, involving all the protagonists and seeking for consensus. If there is no synodality without primacy,[98] the minister who is the leader is making the final decision from this whole spiritual process of listening and discernment that is embodied in the important notion of *conspiratio*.[99] We might consider an image first developed by Cardinal John Henry Newman in the nineteenth century: the *conspiratio fidelium et pastorum*, literally the 'breathing together of the faithful and the pastors'.[100] The journey of synodality is never a solitary adventure, it implies and fosters the ecclesial 'we', but a 'we' integrating all the 'I' in an inclusive approach.

Recalling that *Pastores Dabo Vobis* envisions that priests 'promote the baptismal priesthood of the entire people of God, leading to its full realization',[101] we propose to endorse a vision of power in ministry as 'a generative force ... to liberate freedom'.[102] This pneumatological conception of power is based on Jesus's mission of liberation as servant leader.[103] Yves Congar's ecclesiology and theology of ministry foregrounds service, replacing the binary of 'priesthood-laity' with 'ministers of services-communities'. Thus, this concept of power places God at the centre of his People as he gathers and sends them out into mission.

---

98 Luc Forestier, 'comment gouverner l'Eglise' Marcher ensemble', *Salvator* (2019), 56-60.

99 This correlation promotes that *singularis conspiratio* between the faithful and their Pastors (78), which is an icon of the eternal *conspiratio* that is lived within the Trinity. The Church thus 'constantly moves forward toward the fullness of divine truth until the words of God reach their complete fulfilment in her', International Theological Commission, *Synodality in the Life and Mission of the Church*, (2018).

100 Richard R. Gaillardetz, *By What Authority? A Primer on Scripture, the Magisterium, and the Sense of the Faithful* (Collegeville, MN: Liturgical Press, 2003), 7.

101 John Paul II, *Pastores dabo vobis* 1992).

102 According to the expressions coming from §71 of the Final Document of the Synod of Bishops on Young People, 'In order to undertake a true journey of maturation, the young need authoritative adults. In its etymological meaning, *auctoritas* indicates the capacity for enabling growth; it does not express the idea of a directive power, but of a real generative force.'

103 Yves Congar, *Pour une Église Servante et Pauvre* (Paris: Les Éditions du Cerf, 1963).

Part III – How to further implement this vision of servant leadership in the church?

To reflect and translate into practice this vision of ministry as servant leadership grounded in the *ecclesia,* we need to implement a model of collaborative ministry. Synodality requires collegiality and *vice versa.* True servant leadership focuses on fostering the vocation and liberating the freedom of those they serve and is anchored in a spiritual approach.[104] Discernment calls for a process of mutual listening and pastoral discernment embraces communal discernment. Teamwork in ministry is so fundamental and diversity is a source of creativity. The disciples were sent on mission two by two. Co-ministering within a team of diverse ministers has to become the 'new normal' of a synodal church.

Collaboration is a way to make visible the intrinsic interrelation between the ordained priesthood and the common priesthood of all the baptized according to *Lumen Gentium 10.* It is the way for participation and co-responsibility claimed by synodality that begins with a process of listening and consultation. It is the practical way to recognize that the Holy Spirit is present in everybody and gives to each baptized, no matter what their vocation, diverse charisms.[105]

However, the pathways to collaboration are most of the time neither natural nor easy. To be a good collaborative minister requires good training,[106] a culture of dialogue and self-knowledge. Team collaboration within the diversity of vocations, married, unmarried lay people, priests, and consecrated persons, is challenging but is usually more fruitful. This means getting to know each other,[107] overcom-

---

104 'Collaborative pastoral leadership is profoundly about spiritual leadership'. Daniel Gast and William Clark. 'Collaboration in a Pastoral Key', in *Collaborative Pastoral Leadership,* ed. William Clark and Daniel Gast (Langham, MD: Lexington, 2017), 195-208.

105 'The connection of ministry to personal charism grounds variety', Thomas O'Meara, *Theology of Ministry* (Mahwah, NJ: Paulist, 1999), [rev. ed.], 149.

106 Gast and Clark, ibid.

107 'Collaborative ministry has to be worked at. There is no other way to engage in listening, reflecting, visioning, planning, deciding, implementing and evaluating together except by engaging in deep conversation with each other.' Maureen Kelly, 'The Demands of Collaborative Ministry', in Eamonn Conway, ed., *Priesthood Today: Ministry in a Changing Church,* (Dublin: Veritas, 2013), 27.

ing fears and stereotypes that may exist, and above all, really training every minister in teamwork, team leadership and participatory processes. The Church can learn much from other fields of society such as management sciences and human resource specialists.[108] The key issue here is the initial and on-going formation of ordained and lay ecclesial ministers, including an emphasis on the human formation.[109] The best way to prepare collaborative ministers is surely to train them together.[110] Priestly formation can no longer segregate seminarians in a male only environment cut-off from the world. Men and women, ordained and baptized are called to be formed and work together in mutual enrichment.[111]

The next step is to put into practice this vision of collaborative ministry rooted in a conciliar ecclesiology and a theology of ministry, including how these have been received since Vatican II and also characterized by synodality. Accountability in the Church cannot be a simple transposition or a replica of procedures that exist in civil organizations of society. It has to take into account the specific nature of the Church, which cannot be reduced to a human organization but always has a double human-divine character.

Surely, accountability procedures found in NGOs and companies can give inspiration to the Church in developing suitable procedures. But what is at stake here requires a theological creativity within an approach based on *aggiornamento* and *ressourcement*, listening to this

---

108 Cf Talentheo in France https://www.talentheo.org/ and Leadership Roundtable in the US https://leadershiproundtable.org/ that are lay initiatives to provide to Church Leaders and ministers with training in best practices of management in the service of their mission.

109 Congregation for the Clergy, *The Gift of the Priestly Vocation* (2016).

110 See Boston College Seminar on Priesthood and Ministry for the Contemporary Church, 'To Serve the People of God: Renewing the Conversation on Priesthood and Ministry', *Origins* 48 (27 December 2018), 484-93, and associated texts from *Origins* 49 (16 January 2020), 525-32.

111 As Henri Nouwen testified: 'I was educated in a seminary that made me believe that ministry was essentially an individualistic affair', *In the Name of Jesus*, [New York, NY: Crossroad, 1992], 55].

'When you look at today's church, it is easy to see the prevalence of individualism among ministers and priests.' Ibid., 38.

present world to discern[112] how to nurture adjusted ecclesial paths of accountability, cognizant that power in the Church is received as a gift from God in service of the community.[113] Thus, in a synodal Church where ministers are 'mingling'[114] with all the people, they are intrinsically accountable to this entire body they represent.[115] We need to contribute to this ongoing research. We must identify the best practices and evaluate theologically various experimentations.

If there is a need for a new kind of structure of power in the Church that is aligned with the vision of synodality and collaborative ministry, we have to try to design one. From Congar, we have learned that a true reform in the Church has two steering wheels, the reform of the structures and the personal reform,[116] conversion of culture and men-

---

112 'L'Église utilise librement les possibilités que l'histoire lui offre pour vivre et agir dans le monde, en se réservant, parce qu'elle n'est pas du monde, de laisser de côté ce qui lui a servi un moment, et d'user d'autres à moyens ou de donner d'autres expressions sa vie.' Yves Congar, *Pour une Église Servante et Pauvre* (Paris: Les Éditions du Cerf, 1963),109.

113 'Our first and fundamental consecration is rooted in our Baptism. No one has been baptized a priest or a bishop. They baptized us as lay people and it is the indelible sign that no one can ever erase. It does us good to remember that the Church is not an elite of priests, of consecrated men, of bishops, but that everyone forms the faithful Holy People of God.' Francis, *Letter to Cardinal Marc Ouellet, President of the Pontifical Commission for Latin America* (19 March 2016).

114 *Christus Vivit*, §29; 'Hence we can understand why, when Jesus returned from his pilgrimage to Jerusalem, his parents readily thought that, as a twelve-year-old boy (cf. Lk 2:42), he was wandering freely among the crowd, even though they did not see him for an entire day: "supposing him to be in the group of travellers, they went a day's journey" (Lk 2:44). Surely, they assumed, Jesus was there, mingling with the others, joking with other young people, listing to the adults tell stories and sharing the joys and sorrows of the group. Indeed, the Greek word that Luke uses to describe the group – *synodía* – clearly evokes a larger "community on journey", of which the Holy Family is a part. Thanks to the trust of his parents, Jesus can move freely and learn to journey with others.'

115 'It is the faithful Holy People of God to whom as pastors we are continually called to look, protect, accompany, support and serve. A father cannot conceive of himself without his children.' Francis, *Letter to Cardinal Marc Ouellet, President of the Pontifical Commission for Latin America* (19 March 2016).

116 'Si la réforme de l'Église perd son lien avec la réforme personnelle, elle devient un exercice de discipline par amour de la discipline. Elle n'est plus chrétienne. Une vraie réforme de l'Église doit toujours être dirigée en fin de compte vers la sainteté de vie de ses membres.' John O'Malley, 'Réforme de l'Eglise', *Etudes* (n° spécial Janvier, 2017), 78.

talities. Francis is emphasizing the aspect of personal conversion that is a pastoral conversion. Good structures are not enough. The exercise of power in ministry has to do a lot with personal internal aspects.

> To work collaboratively requires a mature sense of inner authority which enables us to speak our experience truthfully, to say what we really feel ... Deference to authority is not the same as respect. The latter is born out of freedom, the former out of fear.[117]

If you minister in authoritarian ways of exercising the authority, it is often linked to immature affectivity and psychological fragilities. One has to be aware of his or her power of influence;[118] the impact his or her word and acts may have on others and what his or her position in ministry generates as an image of power for the others. That is why reflection and supervision are so important for a healthy minister's leadership style. To minister as 'copartners with the Spirit' is not a mathematical formula but an art.

Conclusion

Laudato Si reminds us that 'everything is connected'. The recent synod on the Amazon has helped to envision how the ecological conversion, the cultural conversion, the pastoral conversion and the synodal conversion are interrelated. As long as human beings promote abusive relationships towards the earth to exploit it, they will have a tendency to develop abusive relationships among themselves and vice versa. Relationships of respect and mutuality between men and women, between people and our planet go hand in hand. The method underlying Laudato Si is the method of dialogue. The vision of this encyclical resonates with the vision of a synodal Church that promotes servant leadership and implements a vision of power in ministry that shuns clericalism and is a generative force of freedom, fostering life and empowering others. Synodality calls us to embrace the ecclesiology of

---

117 Maureen Kelly, 'The Demands of Collaborative Ministry', in Eamonn Conway, ed., *Priesthood Today: Ministry in a Changing Church*, 25-6.
118 Final Document of the Synod on Youth, §130.

Vatican II with fresh insight so that our pastoral practice and shared exercise of ministry can engage with the world in a mutual fecundity. Synodality is not an institution but a process of mutual listening and discernment to the Spirit of surprises.[119]

Questions

- A truly synodal church needs a new understanding and structure of power. How might clericalism impede this reform?

- At the heart of synodality is listening, a mutual listening in which everyone has something to learn. What conditions are necessary for a listening process that will ensure everyone is heard and listened to?

---

119 http://www.vatican.va/content/francesco/en/cotidie/2017/documents/papa-frances-co-cotidie_20170508_god-of-surprises.html

5

SYNODALITY, THE HOLY SPIRIT, AND DISCERNMENT OF SPIRITS

Jos Moons SJ

Jos Moons is a Dutch Jesuit who teaches theology at the Katholieke Universiteit Leuven and the University of Tilburg. Synodality depends upon an understanding of how God is still guiding God's Church. We need to understand this individually and as a Church community. In this chapter Moons discusses the nature of spiritual openness and transparency that are necessary for an authentic experience of discernment. In partiuclar, he focuses upon aspects of (Ignatian) discernment of spirits, especially inner freedom (or detachment) and interiority (or inner movements) as a place of truth.

Jos Moons holds a doctorate from the University of Tilburg on Lumen gentium. In addition to his university teaching he has extensive experience as a pastor and university chaplain. He has recently been appointed to a research group at KU Leuven on synodality.

Synodality is the way forward for Church governance, according to Pope Francis. He dreams of the Church as the people of God on a journey, seeking to hear what the Spirit is saying to the churches in our time. The topic features both in the new format of interviews – the famous 2013 interview by Antonio Spadaro shortly after his election and the recent interview by Austen Ivereigh, published as a book by Ivereigh[120] – and in the more classical form of encyclicals, exhortations, homilies and so on. For example, in his memorable re-flection at the occasion of the 50th anniversary of the Bishops' Synod, Pope Francis stated that 'from the beginning of my ministry as Bishop of Rome, I sought to enhance the Synod, which is one of the most precious legacies of the Second Vatican Council'.[121] For the Pope, this view of the church and of church governance is nothing short of a calling from God.[122]

Now walking this path of synodality is not a goal in itself; the ob-jective is to follow the Spirit's promptings. It is therefore crucial to ask how the Spirit's 'voice' can be heard, all the more so as usually a variety of viewpoints claim to result from listening to the Spirit. In this con-tribution I will first briefly sketch some essential features of synodality, most of which will be treated at greater length elsewhere in this book, and then dwell on Ignatian discernment of spirits as a spiritual tool to sense the Spirit's guiding of the church.

---

120 Antonio Spadaro, 'A Big Heart Open to God: An Interview with Pope Francis', *America Magazine* (30 September 2013); the interview was published simultaneously in various Jesuit journals around the world. Austen Ivereigh, *Let us Dream: The Path to a Better Future. Pope Francis in Conversation with Austen Ivereigh* (London: Simon Schuster, 2020).

121 Address on 17 October 2015, in the context of the Synod on the Family. Online at vatican.va. For extensive discussion, see Massimo Faggioli, 'From Collegiality to Synodality: Promise and Limits of Francis's "Listening Primacy"', *Irish Theological Quarterly*, 85 (2020), 352-369.

122 Cf. from the same address: 'it is precisely this path of synodality which God expects of the Church of the third millennium. What the Lord is asking of us is already in some sense present in the very word "synod". Journeying together — laity, pastors, the Bishop of Rome — is an easy concept to put into words, but not so easy to put into practice'.

Synodality: A very short introduction

Synodality represents a relatively new approach to church governance. Still, it is part of the broad Roman Catholic tradition and can be linked to the style of governance in the early church and in various religious orders. As it is also related to modern developments in relation to secular governance, one could argue that its re-introduction stems both from *ressourcement* and *aggiornamento*.

The Second Vatican Council was a high point of the re-introduction of synodality. Interestingly, it used the term 'synod' to describe itself. In fact, 'council' and 'synod' were used as more or less synonyms. For example, the official title of the minutes of the Council (that includes all the drafts versions of texts and the interventions of Council fathers) uses both the word 'synod' and 'council': *Acta synodalia sacrasancti concilii oecumenici Vaticanii II*. And while the Constitution on the Sacred Liturgy *Sacrosanctum Concilium* (1963) speaks about itself in its opening words as 'This most-holy council', the opening words of the Dogmatic Constitution on the Church *Lumen Gentium* self-qualify the Council as 'this most-holy synod' (1964).

After the Council, various instruments of synodal governance were meant to keep the synodal way going, for example, the Synod of Bishops. In recent times the Bishops gathered in 2014 and 2015 for the Synod on the Family, which was followed by the famous Post-Synodal Apostolic Exhortation on Love in the Family, *Amoris Laetitia* (2016). Other instruments of governance breathe a synodal spirit, too, even though they don't feature the term synod(al). These include the Bishops' Conference, an institution that predated the Council but that was confirmed and received a new vigour in the Decree Concerning the Pastoral Office of Bishops in the Church, *Christus Dominus* (1965),[123] or parish pastoral councils, recommended by the Decree on the Apostolate of the Laity, *Apostolicam Actuositatem* (1965).[124]

---

123 See no. 36-38. cf. 'This sacred ecumenical synod earnestly desires that the venerable institution of synods and councils flourish with fresh vigor' (36) and 'An episcopal conference is, as it were, a council in which the bishops of a given nation or territory jointly exercise their pastoral office' (38).

124 See no. 26. For a more nuanced discussion on parish councils, see Mark Fisher, 'What Was Vatican II's Intent Regarding Parish Councils?', *Studia Canonica* 33 (1999), 5-25.

However, over time the synodal spirit has weakened. Episcopal synodality requires an openness in sharing one's views that is at odds with the culture of following the party line that grew (and was promoted) under post-conciliar papacies. Pope Francis's repeated call for bishops to speak their minds during synods strongly suggests that such was not being done. Similarly bishops' conferences have often lacked the fraternal and dialogical culture that is needed for a synodal way of proceeding, and nowadays pastoral councils often play a marginal role in the functioning of parishes.

This brief overview suggests that true synodality requires two changes.[125] Firstly, it requires a culture change in the church in relation to obedience and 'following the party line'. Without a more positive approach to criticism, dialogue and questions, synodality simply cannot exist. Secondly, for synodality in its richest possible form, a greater inclusion of the laity is required. Both on a practical and theological level their contribution deserves to be better honoured.

The type of synodality advocated here has solid theological roots, the first of which consists in the reality and priority of the Spirit's role. The Spirit is not merely the instrument of Christ or the hierarchy but plays 'his own' active role.[126] Moreover, theologically speaking that role has priority over the hierarchy's leadership role. As it is *ultimately* the Spirit who leads the Church, not the hierarchy, this means practically speaking that all are called to listen to what the Spirit is saying. The hierarchy's role in taking decisions must be situated and lived in the context of the Spirit's leadership role which necessitates facilitating the listening process.

---

125 For arguments similar to what follows here, see Ormond Rush, 'Inverting the Pyramid: the *Sensus Fidelium* in a Synodal Church', *Theological Studies* 78 (2017), 299-325, and Myriam Wijlens, 'Reforming the Church by Hitting the Reset Button: Reconfiguring Collegiality within Synodality because of *sensus fidei fidelium*', *The Canonist* 8 (2017) 235-261. Cf. the International Theological Commission's worthwhile text 'Synodality in the Life and Mission of the Church' (2018), available online.

126 Sound Trinitarian theology advocates *both* that any divine person's 'own' contribution belongs to the one God (so as to protect God's one-ness) and that each person is active (so as to protect God's three-ness). This point needs more elaboration than can be offered here.

A second theological root is the baptismal dignity of the faithful. It implies that the Spirit dwells and works in all the faithful, who constitute together the people of God (*Lumen gentium*, 9-12). The Spirit has not only been given to the bishops – hence, collegiality – but to all the faithful. Here, the old distinction between a hierarchical teaching church and a lay learning church (*ecclesia docens, ecclesia discens*) has been surpassed. Once again, this does not mean that the hierarchy's role is abolished, but recontextualized: the ordained ministers can only discern the Spirit if they have first contemplated the Spirit's (possible) work in the people as a whole.

The third foundational conviction is the theological difference between God and the church (in its general sense of the people of God). Or, to echo the Second Vatican Council, Christ is the light of the peoples, which the church attempts to reflect (*Lumen gentium*, 1). And in pneumatological terms: the Spirit leads the church, which He does by means of ministries and charisms (*Lumen gentium*, 12).[127] Historically, therefore, the church is an eschatological reality: she is a pilgrim people on a journey, constantly trying to reflect Christ's light and to be led by the Spirit. In more concrete terms, that involves conversion, reform, and discerning the signs of the times. Synodality is a means to bring alive the theoretical idea of a pilgrim church.

Discernment

Thus, synodality presupposes that God is still guiding us, not only individually but also as a body, as a people. It is not sufficient to reach back to revelation and tradition, and to apply those, or to talk only about hierarchical leadership; here and now the Holy Spirit guides God's people. If that holds true, then how is one to 'know' where God is leading? How to 'sense' the Spirit's guidance?

Ignatian discernment of spirits is a helpful source in that undertaking, as its aim is precisely that: to discern God's voice and guidance by uncovering and evaluating the various possible 'voices' or

---

127 For the need of both Christ and the Spirit, see John Zizioulas's wonderful essay 'Christ, the Spirit and the Church', in *Being as Communion* (New York: St. Vladimir's Seminary Press, 1985), 123-142.

'inspirations'.[128] I propose to discuss four foundational aspects of discernment: 1) 'Indifference' as the *conditio sine qua non* that creates space for whatever God may be wishing to communicate; 2) An active and affective faith culture that centres around Christ's relevation and the Spirit's inner movements; 3) Grounding our discernment in reality; 4) A dialogical 'way of proceeding'.

Indifference

Firstly, discernment presupposes inner freedom or, in Jesuit jargon, 'indifference'.[129] Indifference is the readiness to give up good things that one likes or wherein one finds God, to contemplate the possibility (or to embrace it) that God may be found also, or more so, in something else. Different from a stoic-like general detachment, indifference concerns every 'disordered' attachment that binds one to anything that is not God. Importantly, indifference is not about sin in our usual understanding of that term; it is a spiritual rather than a moral category. Thus, indifference could be termed 'relational ascetism', for it is because one wishes to preserve or deepen the bond with God that one leaves behind or abstains from something.

An enlightening text in this regard is the 'Principle and Foundation' that forms the basis of the guidelines for meditation in the Spiritual Exercises. Ignatius starts by stipulating that '[t]he human person is created to praise, reverence and serve God our Lord, and by doing so save his or her soul'. After some explanation, he concludes with a description of the corresponding life style that illustrates what detachment is without using the word:

> Thus as far as we are concerned, we should not want health more than illness, wealth more than poverty, fame more than

---

128 Discernment has much older roots than Ignatius of Loyola, see, e.g., Scripture, the desert fathers and mothers, or the Modern Devotion. The Jesuits neither invented it nor own it.

129 For an excellent presentation, see Pierre Emonet, 'Indiferencia', in Javier Melloni a.o. (eds.) *Diccionario de Espiritualidad Ignaciana* (Bilbao/Santander: Mensajero, 2007), 1015-1022.

disgrace, a long life more than a short one, and similarly for all the rest, but we should desire and choose only what helps us more towards the end for which we are created.[130]

Concretely speaking, indifference means giving up one's 'darlings': preferences, wishes, convictions, or anything at all. For example, the reorganisation of dioceses and/or parishes seems a relevant issue in the Irish church at this moment. Whoever is sure that my diocese or parish cannot be reordered (or: must be so) lacks indifference. In vain will he or she attempt to sense God's guidance. For a Synodal process one must be open, so that God can actually suggest things. Whoever is too much 'in the know' and too certain about what is best, can save herself or himself the effort of engaging in any discernment or synodal process; there is simply no point in looking for God if one already knows.[131]

A 'Faith Culture'

Secondly, as a complement to indifference, discernment presupposes some form of 'faith culture'. Once 'darlings' are out of the way, one's thinking and feeling should be informed by faith. This entails some form of prayer, familiarity with the gospel and the church, service, and living Christian virtues such as hope and love. To be sure, faith culture is a much broader category than obedience to magisterial teaching or attending the weekly Eucharist; essentially it concerns one's relationship to God lived at the service of others, which one may do in a variety of ways. For example, while one person likes to pray the rosary or the breviary, another person may prefer silent meditation, or find God in the beauty of nature; all of these qualify as elements of a prayerful faith culture. Similarly, the Eucharistic 'real presence' of Christ must be honoured in the needy also, with the category of 'needy' varying

---

130 Ignatius of Loyola, *The Spiritual Exercises*, no. 23. Here in the translation by Joe Munitiz and Philip Endean, see *Personal writings: Reminiscences, Spiritual Diary, Select Letters including the text of The Spritual Exercises* (Harmondsworth: Penguin books, 1996).

131 It would be interesting to link this with 'negative theology': a theology that acknowledges that God exceeds beyond our comprehension and that we don't know.

from refugees on the move to gay Catholics who feel marginalised in church, or simply one's sick neighbour.[132]

Such a broadly understood faith culture will yield amongst other fruits a 'sense' of or sensitivity for the things of God. When the Second Vatican Council beautifully specified conscience as a place where one personally hears God's voice – 'Conscience is the most intimate centre and sanctuary of a person, in which he or she is alone with God whose voice echoes within them' – it presupposes such a sense.[133] One can also think of the notion of *sensus fidei fidelium*: the sense of faith of the faithful that the Spirit works in us.[134] Largely neglected in magisterial teaching after its rediscovery during the Second Vatican Council, this notion is making somewhat of a comeback in recent years, thanks to the International Theological Commission and Pope Francis.[135]

Yet this sense not only relates to intellectual and rational notions such as 'God's voice that speaks', it runs deeper and includes what Ignatian jargon calls 'inner movements', or, in more simple language, feelings or experience. Discernment of spirits promotes the realm of affectivity as the place where one encounters God. It presupposes that God interacts directly with each human person, that one's interiority (with its inner movements) is a privileged place to become aware of that interaction, and that, by discerning these movements, one is able

132 For another, at times more narrow understanding of such a faith culture, see the International Theological Commission's document 'Sensus fidei in the Life of the Church' (2014), no. 87-126.

133 *Gaudium et Spes*, no. 16, Norbert Tanner (ed.), *Decrees of the Ecumenical Councils* (Washington, DC: Georgetown University Press, 1990).

134 For the importance of the Spirit's role in this regard, cf. Jos Moons, '"Aroused and sustained by the Holy Spirit"? A Plea for a Pneumatological Reconsideration of *Sensus Fidei* on the Basis of *Lumen Gentium* 12', *Gregorianum* 99 (2018), 271-292.

135 For the ITC, see footnote 13. For Pope Francis, see, e.g., Spadaro's interview with Pope Francis (footnote 1) and *Evangelii Gaudium*. Different from the magisterium, the theological world has not neglected the sensus fidei, as the overview articles by John Burkhard illustrate, see his four (!) overview articles 'Sensus Fidei: Theological Reflection Since Vatican II' for the period 1965-2001, published in *The Heythrop Journal* 34 (1993), 46 (2005), and 47 (2006).

to sense what to do.[136] This is not about thinking, but about sensing. In that regard it is interesting too that Ignatius concluded his letters full of detailed instructions often with the wish that the addressee may sense – *sentir* – God's will. Ultimately it was not about Ignatius's directions but God's, and these were not so much known as felt.[137]

Admittedly, the affective realm is a tricky place where deception looms large. Inner peace about a certain idea can be a reliable sign of God, indicating that this is the right thing to say or do, as much as a deceptive peace of, e.g., laziness or shallowness. Zeal can be bitter and cold, or holy and shaking things up. Yet discernment is worth the risk, for what is at stake is God's very guidance. Moreover, the risk of being deceived is as present in any other aspect of faith culture. For example, one may reach out to homeless people out of charity, out of obligation, or to fill one's own inner void.

In short, to know God's will, we need a faith culture. This includes relating to God, growing in familiarity with the person and the life style of Christ, serving others, and engaging in and with the church. Furthermore, a faith culture needs to engage with the affective realm; to be able to sense God's becoming one needs to grow in familiarity with one's inner movements and to learn to discern.

Reality

While discernment has up to this point been described as a spiritual operation, the concrete aspect is in fact equally important. Discernment cannot be done 'in general'. Instead, the spiritual process needs 'incarnation' into reality by means of a clear focus and down-to-earth facts and figures.

Focus means that the issue in relation to which we are trying to sense the Spirit's guidance needs to be specified. To avoid overly general considerations, the issue is best formulated as a question with 'what' or 'how'. For example, 'with the falling numbers of church

---

136 Direct contact, interiority, and sensing are all quintessential elements of Ignatian spirituality. For a succinct presentation and literature, see Jos Moons, *The Art of Spiritual Direction. A Guide to Ignatian Practice* (Dublin: Messenger, 2001), esp. chapter 2, 'Core Values', 17-38.

137 For examples and discussion, see previous footnote.

attendance, what possible future do we foresee for church buildings?'
Or: how to increase the involvement of lay people or the place of
women in the church? Or: what are the most pressing issues to im-
proving the church's credibility in society?

In addition, discernment needs information. Without a certain
knowledge, one's discernment is out of touch. For example, a synodal process on the future of church buildings needs information on
the number of weekly churchgoers per parish, how that number has
developed over the past 50 years, and what sociologists expect for the
(near) future. Similarly for finances, volunteers, priests, bishops, the
structural status of church buildings, and so on. In the same way, a
synodal process on homosexuality needs to engage with the academy:
psychology, moral theology, exegesis. Further, in both cases information must include the 'lived religion' of pastors at the grassroot level as
well as testimonies of those concerned.

Importantly, the spiritual and concrete aspects are complementary
and should be integrated. One needs detachment to be able to welcome information with an open mind. Similarly, sensing the Spirit's
guidance happens not after having received information; rather one
looks out for the 'inner movements' that the information stirs up, and
that one subsequently discerns.

A Dialogical 'Way of Proceeding'

Finally, discernment is not an individual process; it needs the puri-
fication brought about by sharing, questions, suggestions, explora-
tion. That may be done in the form of personal conversation or indeed as part of a communitarian process. After the example of the
'Deliberations of Our First Fathers' on the question if their informal
collaboration needed to become something more solid – a question
that resulted in the founding of the Society of Jesus – Jesuits have
in past decades been experimenting with 'common discernment'.[138]
While I think it is fair to say that we ourselves are still learning how

---

138 For the text, see 'The Deliberation That Started the Jesuits', translated and commen-
    tary by Jules Toner, *Studies in the Spirituality of the Jesuits* 6 (1974), available online,
    https://ejournals.bc.edu/index.php/jesuit/issue/view/378.

it works, the following elements are essential both for common discernment and a synodal process: getting to know one another, clear information, praying together, sharing. The process may well repeat itself on the basis of drafts or plans.

Again, such a dialogical approach needs incarnation, here in the form of method and structure. What is the best way to get to know one another? Informally at a drink or formally, and what about sizeable and diverse groups? What about the actual dialogue; how to share in such groups? And indeed how to share at all – for the 'soft' art of sharing must be preferred over 'tough' discussion, yet people usually tend to the latter. Further issues include processing input and getting feedback on drafts or plans.

While I think we very much need professional expertise about this, the elements identified above matter greatly as well. In my own experience, the main hindrance for common discernment has been various kinds of unfreedom, both in myself and my fellow Jesuits. I expect the same for synodal processes. Indeed, what we have witnessed happening in Rome at synods on various 'hot topics' suggests as much.

Conclusion

Jerónimo Nadal once described Ignatius beautifully as someone 'going with the flow of the Spirit': 'He followed the Spirit, who led the way – he did not himself go in front. Thus he was gently being led, not knowing where to.'[139] The Ignatius portrayed here was not living in Rome, managing a booming and successful new religious order, the Jesuits; this portrait related to his time in Paris, long before the actual founding of the Jesuits. Having left everything without arriving anywhere as yet, he still followed calmly and confidently.

Such an attitude (that partly owes to hagiographic admiration, no doubt) seems very much what one needs for synodal processes. The synodal pilgrimage need pilgrims: people who take the risk of the journey and, as Abram let go of Haran (read: indifference);

---

139 *Monumenta Historica Societatis Iesu*, vol. 73 (Rome: Typis Pontificis universitatis Gregorianae, 1951), 252. Cf the beautiful Latin: 'Tametsi singulari animi modestia ducentem spiritum sequebatur, non praeibat. Itaque deducebatur quo nesciebat suaviter.'

people with a pilgrim's culture (read: faith culture); people who share the journey with fellow pilgrims (read: dialogical way of proceeding). Finally, a pilgrimage needs a focus and some information on the trajectory (read: grounding in reality). Ultimately the pilgrim's attitude is a way of professing the faith. It witnesses to a deep belief that the church is the people of God on a pilgrimage and to a deep faith in the Spirit's person and guidance.

Questions

- *Discernment is a crucial element of a successful synodal process. Are there perhaps some pre-synodal preparations to be done to ensure that the Holy Spirit will be listened to? Do we know enough about the process of discernment and if not how can we prepare for it?*

- *Our pilgrim journey involves conversion, reforms and discerning the signs of the times. How can we recreate a 'Road to Emmaus' experience where Jesus walked with the downcast disciples as he listened intently to them?*

6

'IT SEEMED GOOD TO THE HOLY SPIRIT AND TO US': SYNODALITY AND DISCERNMENT IN ACTS 15

Jessie Rogers

Jessie Rogers lectures in Scripture at St Patrick's College Maynooth where she is also Dean of the Faculty of Theology. In this chapter she unpacks the account of the Council at Jerusalem in the Acts of the Apostles and the events leading up to it to glean insights into how the Holy Spirit guided the Church toward the radical decision to accept non-Jewish members without requiring circumcision and Torah observance. The communal process of discernment included listening to testimony about divine action in the world; hearing disparate voices and opinions; reflecting on Scripture in light of experience; and arriving at an agreed position articulated by the apostles. A reflection on this early Church experience can be helpful to the Church as it embraces synodality today.

Dr Rogers is trained in Ignatian spiritual accompaniment and contributed to the facilitation of the discernment process in the recent diocesan synods in Limerick and Liverpool.

When we search for a biblical perspective on synods and synodality, it makes good sense to turn to Acts 15, the account of
how the early Church came to a decision about a very contentious
issue that fundamentally shaped its identity. What has become known
as the Council of Jerusalem played a key role in the growth of the
Church from being a small movement within Judaism solely centred
on Jerusalem into a global religion open to people of every culture.

Acts devotes a lot of space to detailing the journey leading to a decision that would have already been known and probably universally
accepted by its first readers. The aim of the narrative is not to convince
its hearers of the decisions reached, but to communicate the process
that led to those decisions. It tells the story in a way that highlights
the practice of communal discernment. I am convinced that Scripture
is revelatory, and that by paying attention to the text itself and to
how the text illuminates life, we will hear God's word spoken into
our own situation. As readers, therefore, we do not simply learn what
happened. We are invited to reflect on the Holy Spirit at work in the
time of the Apostles so that we can recognise the same Spirit at work
in the Church today. When we read it alert to hints of praxis, we can
discover much to help us in our own synodal journey.

In Acts 14, Paul and Barnabas completed their first missionary journey
and returned to the church in Antioch which had sent them to spread the
Gospel. We first hear of the community of Christians in Antioch in Acts
11, but to understand just how radical they were, we need to return to
the beginning of Acts. After Jesus's resurrection and before his ascension,
he told the disciples: 'you will receive power when the Holy Spirit has
come upon you; and you will be my witnesses in Jerusalem, in all Judea
and Samaria, and to the ends of the earth' (Acts 1:8).[140] The Holy Spirit
came upon the nascent community at Pentecost and empowered them to
witness. The Church began to grow in Jerusalem, but it did not spread
beyond there until persecution scattered the believers further afield. The
apostles, however, remained in Jerusalem.

---

140 All quotations are from the New Revised Standard Version.

Now those who were scattered because of the persecution that took place over Stephen travelled as far as Phoenicia, Cyprus, and Antioch, and they spoke the word to no one except Jews. But among them were some men of Cyprus and Cyrene who, on coming to Antioch, spoke to the Hellenists also, proclaiming the Lord Jesus. The hand of the Lord was with them, and a great number became believers and turned to the Lord (Acts 11:19-21).

The first followers of Jesus were Jewish and they had come to believe that Jesus was the long-awaited Jewish messiah. Initially, all those who joined them were Jewish. It did not occur to them that the Good News was not just for Jesus's own people, but for the whole world. But those who ended up in Antioch had a greater vision. They also told their new non-Jewish neighbours about Jesus, and many of these also joined the community. In Antioch what we today might call 'lay-led ministry' crossed a boundary that the Church as a whole had not considered transgressing. The account of the conversion of the Roman centurion Cornelius (Acts 10) illustrates just how strong the barrier was that existed between Jew and Gentile in the understanding of the first Jewish Christians. Peter needed to be given a vision and hear a voice saying, 'What God has made clean, you must not call profane' (Acts 10:15) three times before he was willing to go to a Gentile's house. Only when the Holy Spirit came upon the Gentile household in the same way as had happened at Pentecost did he realise that, since God accepted them, he could not withhold baptism from them (Acts 10:44-48). God is very active in pushing for this encounter – sending an angel to Cornelius to direct him to Peter and unsettling Peter's inbuilt resistance through the threefold vision before giving the Holy Spirit to the Gentiles in an incontestable way. A lot of unlearning must happen before the apostles catch up with what God is doing.

By contrast, those who arrive in Antioch seem to be doing what comes naturally to them. So great is their enthusiasm for Jesus Christ that they cannot help but witness to their neighbours, whatever the background. We are first of all told of their missionary activity, and only afterwards that the hand of the Lord was with them as seen in the response of the people. Their faith instinct has guided them reliably.

This is the sensus fidei, the sense of faith, at work, as they know instinctively what their faith requires of them in a new situation. When the Church in Jerusalem hears of this, they send Barnabas, 'a good man, full of the Holy Spirit and of faith' (Acts 11:24) to check it out. He can recognise that this is the grace of God at work, and encourages them to continue, bringing in Paul, still called Saul, to strengthen them further (Acts 11:26).

The Church's boundaries extend to include Gentiles, but some in Judea become uncomfortable with the ease with which these new converts are being incorporated into the people of God. They cannot argue with God that there is space at the table for the Gentiles, but surely these newcomers have to observe the boundary marker of circumcision to become part of God's people? By the time of the events recounted in Acts 15, the question is not whether Gentiles can become part of the Jesus movement but rather how their incorporation in the people of God was to be marked and the degree to which their Christian identity was also to be Jewish. There were a number of distinct and diverse groupings within Judaism in the first century CE, but all of them held in common the practice of male circumcision. The only Jews in this period opposed to circumcision were 'secularists' who wanted to hide their Jewish identity because it was a hindrance to getting on in the world.

From our perspective it may seem like those in favour of circumcision were the legalists who were seeking to impose an additional burden on Gentile converts. But theirs, in fact, was the position with precedent and tradition on its side. Jesus and his earliest followers were all Jewish, and to claim that Jesus was the Messiah was to make a Jewish claim about the fulfilment of Jewish expectations. Genesis 17 recounts that Abraham, the ancestor of Israel and the first proselyte, was given the sign of circumcision. What is more, this 'covenant in the flesh' was to be an everlasting covenant that applied also to the foreigners who were included in Abraham's household – in his case through being bought as slaves – and 'any uncircumcised male who is not circumcised in the flesh of his foreskin shall be cut off from his people; he has broken my covenant' (Gen 17:13-14). Therefore, when the Jesus movement spread beyond the Jewish people to include Gentiles and it became clear that

God by the Holy Spirit was including them in the people of God, it was not unreasonable to assume that the boundary marker of circumcision should still apply. After all, by being 'in Christ', the Gentiles were being included in the people of God and therefore in Abraham's household of faith. It was the evolving practice of circumcision-free mission to Gentiles that was taking the early Church into brand new territory and setting a new precedent.

All of this is at play when 'certain individuals came down from Judea [to Antioch] and were teaching the brothers that "unless you are circumcised according to the custom of Moses, you cannot be saved"' (Acts 15:1). This intervention causes dissension in the community, with Paul and Barnabas debating in favour of the opposing position. It is ironic that a question about salvation, which is healing and a return to wholeness, produces disunity and consternation in the community.

Debate does not solve the issue so the decision is made to take the question to the apostles and elders in Jerusalem (Acts 15:2). This choice may be because the proponents of the dissenting position are from Judea but it is more likely because the authority of the Jerusalem leadership is recognised. The Gospel has gone out from there, and it is to this authoritative source that Paul and Barnabas and their companions make their journey as delegates of the church in Antioch. On the way, the delegation testifies by recounting at length the conversion of the Gentiles, eliciting a response of 'great joy' (Acts 15:3) from the believers. This joy, shared by all, is in sharp contrast to the dissension caused by the intervention of the proponents of circumcision earlier. In Acts, joy is the response to discerning the Holy Spirit at work or the coming of God's Kingdom (cf. Acts 8:8 and 13:52). That the believers who host the delegation on their journey respond with joy is the fruit of the sensus fidelium, the intuitive recognition by the faithful that the story of the conversion of the Gentiles is the story of God at work in a new way.

Having been sent by the church in Antioch, the delegation is received by the church and the apostles and elders in Jerusalem; there is welcome and mutual recognition. Those from Antioch do not come with propositions or arguments for a particular position; they 'reported all that God had done with them' (Acts 15:4). By telling their story they bear witness to God's work in the world, a testimony which has already elicited joy in other believers.

Then the opposing position is heard. Those who take the alternative view are described as believers belonging to the sect of the Pharisees (Acts 15:5). They are a part of the Church but characterised by their distinctiveness. The position they advocate would have been the un-reflective opinion of most in Jerusalem, because they would have had no reason to question it. So, the two sides, the two stories and the two interpretations of God's work of salvation in the world have been set out clearly. The believing Pharisees appeal to law and custom. The Antioch delegation tells the story of what God has been doing.

Until that story is heard, there would have been very little in the experience of the elders and apostles to date to cause them to question what they took to be self-evident, viz., the continuing validity of the Mosaic law for all believers. Now they need to discern. The transla-tion: 'The apostles and elders met together to consider this matter' (Acts 15:6) does not do justice to the task at hand. Literally, they are gathered together to 'see' (idein) about this matter. What is required is a careful seeing, in other words, a true discernment. They don't just have to hear what is said and then apply what they already know. They must begin by looking closely.

That discernment does not come about as some sort of mystical knowing or charismatic revelation. There is 'much debate' (Acts 15:7), implying that all sides are being heard as various positions are argued for. The debate does not lead to breakthrough, though, until Peter stands up and reminds them of how God had saved the household of Cornelius. He appeals to what they know from 'the early days' which is therefore not a new innovation. Nevertheless, the surprising shift that God had so clearly insisted that Peter make at that juncture has continuing repercussions which they are only now beginning to un-derstand more fully. God had made it clear that he did not make a distinction between Jew and Gentile (Acts 15:9). Those pushing for circumcision wanted to say that God does not discriminate, in that God requires everyone to be circumcised. But the action of the Spirit in the conversion of Cornelius has forced a different conclusion. There is no distinction because Jewish Christians are saved in the same way as Gentile Christians! The unity of salvific experience happens the other way around. The story of what God is doing among the Gentiles provides a lens through which the Jewish Christians can better articulate their own experience. In wrestling with this issue, the Church is not simply working toward a practical decision; she is deepening her understanding of the faith and growing her theology.

Something shifts in the gathering at this point because, instead of debating, 'the whole assembly kept silence, and listened' (Acts 15:12). They are on the cusp of the 'overflow' that Pope Francis speaks of in *Let Us Dream*, the new understanding which becomes possible when we hold to rather than dissipate the tensions, listen deeply, and do not resolve the matter too quickly.[141] This silence holds the potential to yield new insight. Silence is not just a space where one lets the other speak while formulating one's own response. It is a space for deep listening. In genuine listening, the space is opened up for movement, for conversion, for change. This listening silence falls on the whole assembly, no longer factions arguing different perspectives, but one body recognising that the Spirit is speaking through the words they are hearing.

Peter's intervention has given those assembled new ears to rehear the witness of Paul and Barnabas. Once again we see the power of testimony. When God is doing a new thing one has to watch, listen, and be open. One cannot predict God's action in the world by arguing from first principles, at least not how these are currently being interpreted. The starting point is to notice where God is at work. Because the assembly has some knowledge already of how God has been at work among them, they have a reference point to recognise it happening in unexpected places too.

Then it is the turn of James, the leader of the church in Jerusalem. Having listened to the point where he has seen deeply into the situation, James is ready to bring reality to scripture for discernment. Acknowledging God at work in the world as described through the interpreted experience of Peter, he picks up where 'this agrees with the words of the prophets' (Acts 15:15) in a passage from the book of

---

141 Austin Ivereigh, *Let Us Dream. The Path to a Better Future. Pope Francis in Conversation with Austin Ivereigh* (London: Simon and Schuster, 2020) 78-83.

Amos. This is not an a priori argument from Scripture, where biblical principles can be known in the abstract and then applied logically to a present situation. Instead, discerning God at work in a surprising way among the Gentiles unlocks the key to seeing this Scripture in a new way. There are depths in the prophecy that can only be understood in retrospect. If one begins with the prophecy in Amos, it is hard to interpret it as referring to anything other than the restoration of Israel as that had been expected by the disciples before the ascension of Jesus when they asked: 'Lord, is this the time when you will restore the kingdom to Israel?' (Acts 1:8). It is only through reflection on historical events and glimpsing the Spirit of God at work therein that a different and richer fulfilment is discerned.

At this point, James is ready to formulate a judgement of the situation and to suggest a way forward (Acts 15:19). This is not a democratic decision, but a discerned one that has the consent of the whole church (Acts 15:22, 25). The decision reached is not the last word on the subject, but it allowed the Gentile Christians in Antioch to live out their freedom in Christ while preserving the unity of the community. That it was a good decision is confirmed by the joy with which it was received in Antioch (Acts 15:31), another instance of the sensus fidelium at work.

To conclude, I would like to reiterate some of the principles of synodality and communal discernment that surface from my reading of Acts 15. First and foremost, the deliberations and decisions of this first Church Council are predicated on the conviction that God is at work in the world and that God is doing something new and surprising. In this particular instance, the mission to the Gentiles is clearly God's work, and the giving of the Spirit to those Gentiles without incorporation into Judaism through circumcision is a fact of their experience. It is surely theologically uncontroversial to claim that the right direction for the Church is the one in which God is moving already. What is theologically and theoretically incontestable – that we must follow where God leads – is more tricky in practice. It requires reading the signs of the times, and reading experience, Scripture and tradition in such a way that we can actually recognise God's footprints.

The text reveals that the people of God can know what God is inviting them to. Discernment is a task for all God's people. The leaders have a vital role to play in listening to and reflecting on the experience of the people of God. Their task is not to argue from theory for a particular position, but to discern from the experience of the people of God in light of precedent and Scripture. But the direction of the movement is interesting! It is not the leaders who know and then communicate that knowledge to the people. The church in Antioch took the initiative, first when its founders took the unprecedented step of sharing the Gospel with Gentiles, and then in sending Barnabas and Paul to Jerusalem with the controversy over circumcision. The elders and apostles interpreted, decided and pronounced before communicating their decision to all the people, where it was received with great joy. The decision resonates with the people whose joy confirms its rightness. There are different roles and responsibilities but, even though James formulates the decision, it is the leadership as a whole, with the consent of the whole church, who communicate it.

The role of testimony, of hearing one another's stories, is striking. There was debate about issues, both in Antioch and in Jerusalem. This debate was only able to move forward to resolution, however, when Peter stood up to retell his story. Real listening happened when stories were told. Listening together to these stories took the issue beyond argument and counter-argument to the real possibility for new and deeper insight.

The process of discovering God's will for a practice which fundamentally shaped the identity of the Church into the future was messy and gradual. The leading of the Spirit happened both as a practice on the margins (Antioch) and through the radical conversion of a key figure – Peter – at the centre. It took time for the issue to emerge and it was controversy that brought it to a head and set it on the rocky road toward resolution. If everything had been formally resolved with a definitive pronouncement from Jerusalem at the very beginning of the Gentile mission, there would have been no lived experience and development to reflect upon. There is a time for living without certainty, for being in process. When the stories which have emerged at the margin and the centre have taken shape and come together through mutual witness and listening, the way forward opens up.

I find the affective dimensions reflected in the narrative quite striking, particularly the silence that accompanies discernment and the joy that recognises the rightness of something. But that is not to downplay the importance of being disturbed or of holding the tension until God's way forward can be discerned. The contrary voices bring the divisions out into the open where they can be reflected on. Even bitter, potentially divisive views need to be heard. The silence that descends implies a deep listening. What begins in argument shifts toward resolution and new insight by means of testimony.

The Church is called to follow God into the world and to do this together as the people of God. We are being invited to rediscover a more synodal way in which we keep in step with each other by keeping in step with the Spirit (cf. Gal 5:25). We come to know the dance of the Spirit as we listen – to experience, to others, to Scripture and tradition, and as we keep our eyes open to reality. What is needed is not rational argument and debate, on the one hand, nor a charismatic 'knowing' that is independent of the hard work of looking and listening to the real on the other. The Church is neither a democracy nor a dictatorship. It is the body of Christ being led by the Spirit towards the future that God creates. Synodal decision-making seeks what seems good to the Holy Spirit and to us (Acts 15:28) as we journey this path together.

Questions:

- In Antioch a 'lot of unlearning had to happen before the apostles catch up with what God is doing'. To what extent is the same true for our church today and what framework do we need to begin that journey?

- There is a time for living without certainty, for being in process. To what extent is the Church in Ireland equipped to deal with uncomfortable truths that are likely to emerge during the synodal process?

7

THE 'SENSE OF FAITH' AND SOME CONTESTED ISSUES

Gerry O'Hanlon SJ

Gerry O'Hanlon is an Irish Jesuit priest and theologian. In this chapter he explains the nature, scope and receptivity function of the sensus fidei fidelium, which is central to the synodal way outlined by Pope Francis. He shows how listening to this 'sense of faith' may help to resolve several contested issues in the everyday life of contemporary Catholicism in Ireland.

Dr O'Hanlon lectured for several years at the Milltown Institute, Dublin. He has written extensively on Church reform and on the role of the Church in the public square. His latest book is *The Quiet Revolution of Pope Francis – A Synodal Catholic Church in Ireland?* (Dublin: Messenger, 2019, revised edition).

In deciding to embark on a 'synodal pathway' for the Irish Catholic Church the Bishops have been inspired by the teaching and practice of Pope Francis. Francis, for his part, has developed the teaching of the Second Vatican Council on collegiality (between the Pope and Bishops) to embrace the wider and deeper notion of synodality, which involves not just the Bishops but all the faithful.

In his most concentrated treatment of synodality (50th Anniversary Address of the Synod of Bishops, 2015) Francis refers back to the Council (Lumen gentium, 12) and its observation that:

> The whole body of the faithful, who have an anointing that comes from the holy one (cf. I Jn 2: 20, 27), cannot err in matters of belief. This characteristic is shown in the supernatural sense of the faith (sensus fidei) of the whole people of God, when "from the bishops to the last of the faithful" it manifests a universal consensus in matters of faith and morals.

These, Francis, adds, 'are the famous words infallible "in credendo" (infallible in believing)'. In this same address he also refers back to his own 2013 Apostolic Exhortation Evangelii Gaudium (see EG, 119-126) and his contention that 'all the baptized, whatever their position in the Church or their level of instruction in the faith, are agents of evangelization' so that 'the sensus fidei prevents a rigid separation between an Ecclesia docens (a teaching Church) and an Ecclesia discens (a learning Church), since the flock likewise has an instinctive ability to discern the new ways that the Lord is revealing to the Church'.

Australian theologian Ormond Rush argues that in effect Francis is making moves towards a synthesis between two notions which are in dramatic tension – the infallibility of the magisterium (Pope and bishops) in teaching, and the infallibility of the People of God in believing. The linchpin linking the two infallibilities, according to Rush, is listening to the sensus fidelium, the people of God's intuition in matters of faith and morals. And so, Rush argues, 'the sensus fidelium, and listening to the sensus fidelium, lie at the heart of Francis's dynamic notion of a synodal church'.[142]

It seems to me that this emphasis on the 'sense of faith', always in dialogue with theology and with the authoritative magisterium, has great potential to unlock some contested issues in the Irish and wider church which are real obstacles to evangelization. First, then, I will

142 Ormond Rush, 'Inverting the Pyramid: The *Sensus Fidelium in a Synodal Church*', *Theological Studies*, 78 (2), 2017, 299-325 at 311-312.

explain in more detail the nature and scope of the 'sense of faith', and then explore its relevance to our contemporary mission.

Nature and scope of the 'sense of faith'.

The 2014 document, *'Sensus Fidei' in the Life of the Church' (SF)*, by the International Theological Commission provides an accessible account of current mainline thinking on the topic. The authors note (1-4) that the sensus fidei, as participation of all the baptised in the prophetic office of Jesus Christ, refers to two realities which are distinct though closely connected: the personal capacity of the believer to discern the truth of faith *(sensus fidei fidelis),* and the communal and ecclesial reality through which the baptized converge in recognizing and endorsing authentic Christian doctrine and practice in the lived reality of today *(sensus fidei fidelium and consensus fidelium).*

Furthermore, the *sensus fidei fidelis* is 'a sort of spiritual instinct that enables the believer to judge spontaneously whether a particular teaching or practice is or is not in conformity with the Gospel and with apostolic faith' (49). This 'instinct' – also described as knowledge of the heart (as between friends), a 'second nature', a 'sixth sense', a 'flair' or 'intuition' – is connatural, immediate and spontaneous, and of a different order than objective knowledge, which proceeds by way of conceptualisation and reasoning and is a result of rational deliberation (49-55, 70). The deeper one's faith and holiness, the more reliable this 'sense of faith' is (56-59). At the communal level (sensus fidei fidelium) the sense of faith enables believers to discern the 'signs of the times' in a way that is both prospective and retrospective (reception): it 'gives an intuition as to the right way forward amid the uncertainties and ambiguities of history, and a capacity to listen discerningly to what human culture and the progress of the sciences are saying' (70). Its scope includes moral as well as doctrinal developments (72-73). Because the sense of faith can also be accompanied by elements of erroneous human opinion, there is often need for considerable time, patience and respect until a conclusive discernment is arrived at, with the faithful at large, bishops and theologians all having their respective roles to play (71), the magisterium having the ultimate authoritative voice (77). It is the same Holy Spirit who is present to all the baptised, in that pastorum et fidelium conspiratio (the breathing together of the pastors and faithful) of which Newman spoke (39).

Liturgy is a particularly rich source of the sense of faith (75), as are popular religion and the poor (82-3, 107-112; EG, 122f, 198). The validity of the contribution does not depend on education or theological background, although theology provides a valuable service in explaining the sense of faith with greater clarity and precision (84). Correct dispositions for a more authentic participation in the sensus fidei include openness to reason and inner freedom and humility (88-105). And, it is noted, 'vast multitudes of Christian believers (and indeed of people beyond the visible bounds of the Church) have privileged access, at least potentially, to the deep truths of God' (109). Thus, as is clear from Vatican II's Gaudium et Spes, the Church learns from as well as teaches the 'world' (GS, 40-44), and the 'sense of faith' is formed not just by inner-church realities but also by a discerning integration of secular history and culture.

Finally, and crucially for our purposes, the document notes that the 'sense of faith' is not simply identical with majority public opinion, sociological data, opinion polls or the 'spirit of the age' (47, 83,87,113-126, especially 118). Nonetheless, SF also notes that 'public exchange of opinion is a prime means by which, in a normal way, the sensus fidelium can be gauged' (125). Therefore, since the 'sense of faith' is so important, since 'it must be recalled that the experience of the Church shows that sometimes the truth of the faith has been conserved not by the efforts of theologians or the teaching of the majority of bishops but in the heart of believers' (119), the faithful need to be consulted appropriately. The normal way of this consultation is by constant communication and dialogue within the Church and, within this, 'public opinion is an important form of that communication in the Church' (124). The authors go on to note that various institutional instruments (councils and synods are mentioned) may also be used to formally hear and consult the faithful – and this, of course, is the point at which we have now arrived at in the Church in Ireland.

So, while public opinion is not determinative on its own, it has an important function. Furthermore, as seems clear in Ireland and elsewhere today, where reception of official teaching meets with 'difficulty and resistance', then the 'magisterium must likewise reflect on the teaching … and consider whether it needs clarification or reformulation' (80). This can happen when 'the majority of the faithful remain indifferent to doctrinal or moral decisions taken by the magisterium or when they positively reject them' (123) – this situation may reveal a weakness or lack of faith on the part of the people of God, but 'in some cases it may indicate that certain decisions have been taken by those in authority without due consideration of the experience and the sensus fidei of the faithful, or without sufficient consultation of the faithful by the *magisterium*' (123).

Contested Issues in Ireland Today

SF, as we have seen, does not shirk from describing controversial contexts in which the 'sense of the faith' clashes in one way or another with official Church teaching. We have experiences of this in the Ireland of today, most obviously with respect to Church teaching on sexuality and gender. The Irish Bishops reported that the findings of their questionnaire to Irish Catholics in preparation for the Roman Synod on the Family revealed that many found the teaching in this area was 'disconnected from real-life experience', and that 'many … expressed particular difficulties with the teachings on extra-marital sex and cohabitation by unmarried couples, divorce and remarriage, family planning, assisted reproduction, homosexuality. The church's teaching in these sensitive areas is often not experienced as realist, compassionate or life-enhancing' (Statement of the Irish Catholic Bishops' Conference, 13 March, 2014).

Two years earlier the Association of Catholic Priests had commissioned Amarach to conduct a survey of Catholic opinion which found that 75% believed that Catholic teaching on sexuality was not relevant to themselves or their families; that three out of five Catholics disagreed with the teaching that any sexual expression of love between gay couples is immoral; 87% believed priests should be allowed to marry, while 77% believed that women should be ordained to the priesthood (*Irish Examiner, 13 April, 2012*).

The Bishops, for their part, pledged in response to the question-naire findings to 'present faithfully the church's teaching on marriage and the family in a positive and engaging way, whilst showing com-passion and mercy towards those who are finding difficulty in accept-ing or living it'. This assumes that the teaching itself is correct and more effective communication and merciful application will solve the problem. However, as we have seen in SF, there is also the possibility that indifference or resistance to the teaching is grounded in a 'sense of the faith' which may indicate that the teaching has been adopted without sufficient consultation and needs to be not just clarified but reformulated.

The stakes are high here – the Catholic Church does not lightly go down the path of doctrinal revision, and there is danger of divi-sion, and even a version of the 'culture wars' we see so prevalent in the United States. And yet most would admit that when teaching in such intimate areas as sex and gender are disregarded, coupled with an already damaged moral credibility of the clerical Church due to the abuse issue, there occurs a significant obstacle to faith and to the mis-sion of the Church. Pope Francis wants to make the Church 'attrac-tive' – for many young people and women in Ireland today it is not attractive. These are 'signs of the time' which need to be addressed. Can we envisage, then, a way of going about this that is true to the Church's own self-understanding? Let me offer some examples, which are sourced in magisterial attention to the 'sense of faith'.

Some recent case studies

European Jesuit theologian, the late Philippe Bacq, succinctly outlines a now uncontroversial, highly instructive, case of recent change in the Catholic Church.[143] For close on two thousand years the Church, in line with secular society, taught there was a natural hierarchy within the family, according to which the husband ruled over the wife, whose duty it was to obey. To support this teaching appeal was made to natu-ral reason, to Scriptural texts in Genesis (2 and 3) and Paul (1 Cor 11:

---

143 Philippe Bacq, 'La relation home-femme dans la societe occidentale et la tradition de l'Eglise', *En Question, 110, (September 2014), 27-29.*

3; Ephesians 5: 22-24), and to authoritative Patristic (Ambrose and Augustine) and Scholastic (Aquinas) sources. The teaching was stated forcefully as late as 1941 by Pius XII, echoing sentiments by Pius XI to the effect that this natural hierarchy could never be changed. However, the cultural evolution of the twentieth century around the dignity and equality of the individual had its effect, not just in civil law but also in Church teaching. By the time of the Second Vatican Council (see GS 49), the Church was stressing the equality of both partners in marriage, founded on a relationship of freedom and mutuality. No reference was made to the previous teaching or to the Scriptural and traditional texts which undergirded it: now it was the Canticle of Canticles that was quoted and a text in Paul (I Cor, 7: 3-6) which focused on reciprocity. Fast forward another 20 years or so and John-Paul II in *Mulieris Dignitatem* (1988) reiterated the teaching of Vatican II and went on to reinterpret the traditional texts which had been used to assert the superiority of man over woman. Due to a cultural evolution, then, the Church was able to reinterpret a teaching which it had long thought to be irreformable: 'L'Eglise peut donc changer sa doctrine meme si, a un moment de son histoire, elle la pensait irreformable' (29).

In a somewhat similar fashion North American theologian Edward Hahnenberg argues that the proliferation of ministries after Vatican II, in particular in the N. American church, is less a product of Vatican II's teaching on the laity and more a response to particular cultural developments and the pastoral needs they generated.[144] In this sense lay ministry was an anomaly, like many other such developments in the church (he references the monoepiscopate, communal forms of monasticism, presbyteral authority, papal primacy, mendicant orders and active communities of women religious), which were more often than not experienced not as natural evolutions but rather as deeply contested innovations and disruption. This often led not only to theological discovery but as a major impetus to doctrinal development, which lead over time to the mainstream theological tradition

144 Edward P. Hannenberg, 'Learning from Experience: Attention to Anomalies in in a Theology of Ministry', in Richard R. Gaillardetz and Edward P. Hannenberg, eds., *A Church with Open Doors* (2015), Collegeville, Minnesota, Liturgical Press, 159-180.

not simply rejecting prior theory but finding 'ways to revise the theory in the light of the exception' (172).

Reflection on these cases

In all of these cases (and of course there are many others too) we have an influence of the 'sense of faith' (often discerned through the influence of contemporary culture) which, over time, the magisterium has been able to accept as an instance of doctrinal development. This is despite the initially seeming disruptive nature of the development proposed, the underlying intelligibility of which theology has learned to locate more precisely within the overall Christian tradition.

It remains the case, however, that the Catholic Church is cautious, almost to the point of denial, about developments which seem at variance with previous teaching. And so, in the Synod on the Family, we had a chorus of voices affirming that what was involved in the possible admission of divorced and remarried to Eucharistic reception that was pastoral/disciplinary in nature, not doctrinal. Pope Francis himself can sometimes seem to suggest this position himself – and so, for example, he says: 'Speaking of synodality, it's important not to confuse Catholic doctrine and tradition with the Church's norms and practices. What is under discussion at synodal gatherings are not traditional truths of Christian doctrine. The Synod is concerned mainly with how teaching can be lived and applied in the changing contexts of our times' (*Let Us Dream, 84-5)*.[145] No doubt it was words like these, coupled with the instinct to be reticent about doctrinal development of a seemingly disruptive nature, which persuaded the Irish Catholic Bishops to state on their synodal website that according to Pope Francis, 'Synods are not instruments to change Church teaching but rather help to apply it more pastorally'.

However, Francis is not quite so absolute on this issue as it might seem at first glance: he is referring only to 'traditional' truths of Christian doctrine (what counts as 'traditional'?) and says the Synod is concerned 'mainly' (not exclusively) with how teaching can be lived.

145 Pope Francis, in conversation with Austen Ivereigh. *Let Us Dream, 2020*, London, Simon & Shuster.

After all, this is the same Francis who has also stated in his *Motu Proprio Spiritus Domini* (15 January 2021) that the change in Canon Law permitting women to be lectors and acolytes represents a 'doctrinal development … arrived at in these last years that has brought light to how certain ministries instituted by the Church have as their basis the common condition of being baptised and the royal priesthood received in the Sacrament of Baptism'. In an accompanying letter he notes that this development occurred due to a number of Assemblies of the Synod of Bishops and cites in particular the Final Document of the Amazon Synod. This case in point, of course fits in well with Hannenberg's thesis of anomalies and exceptions leading to doctrinal development, and historically many other examples could be cited. Francis is too astute theologically not to know this – doctrine develops, teaching changes, and often due to synodal assemblies and councils through which the 'sense of faith' of the faithful is formally and authoritatively discerned – and so Francis can also say: 'Tradition is not a museum, teaching changes, and doctrine is not static but grows and develops' (*Let Us Dream,* 57).

The Bishops, with Francis, are right to be wary of division, of an exclusively 'parliamentary procedure' which does not rise to the level of discernment, of the 'isolated conscience' and single-issue reform mentality which can easily sow a partisan and sectarian spirit. But it's also true that discernment can be 'noisy',[146] can integrate and purify vigorous debate and conflict, lobbying and gossip – we are human beings, not angels! Interestingly, Francis himself noted of the Amazon Synod that while it could not in the end rise to the level of discernment on the contested issues of married priests and female deacons (a sign of which was that, unlike in the Synod on the Family, the different sides remained as fixed in their views at the end of the process as they had been at the beginning), nonetheless what occurred was a 'rich, productive and even necessary parliament'.[147] And so, he is saying, let the debate continue, let us ask God's grace to raise it to the

---

146 Gerry O'Hanlon, *The Quiet Revolution of Pope Francis,* 2018/9, Dublin, Messenger Publications, chapters 6 and 5.

147 Antonio Spadaro, 'Francis's Government: What is the driving force of his pontificate?', *La Civilta Cattolica,* 5 September 2020, 4.

level of true communal discernment, so that the urgent questions it addresses may soon be resolved.

Some of these issues surrounding the more precise nature of Synods and Assemblies and their role in doctrinal development may well feature on the agenda for the Rome Synod on Synodality in 2022, towards which our own consultative process in Ireland will contribute. Meanwhile, however, we cannot ask Catholics in Ireland to enter a lengthy consultative process, investing themselves in this synodal pathway, and, at the same time, tell them that they can't speak their minds, can't exercise that *parrhesia* (boldness of speech) which Pope Francis so constantly recommends. This would be counter-productive. We are looking to discern the 'sense of faith', confident that it is there we find the leadings of the Holy Spirit, and we need to take all means to ensure that this happens. It is certainly true that on contested issues like the ones mentioned, we all need to be patient as well as engaged: these issues affect not just the Irish but the universal Church, and must await an authoritative final judgement from the universal church. Nonetheless what happens in Ireland can be of enormous significance in bringing about the kind of judgement and teaching which can be received in peace by the faithful, when the conclusions of the Irish discernment are fed into the wider Church.

The Road to Emmaus

Initially there was a rather muted and sometimes fearful response to the announcement by the Bishops of a synodal pathway for the Irish Church. Perhaps that was to be expected: like the two disciples on the road to Emmaus (Lk 24: 13-35), Catholics in Ireland are demoralised, for many good reasons. And yet, as the two disciples discovered, on the way, meeting and talking with the Stranger, their desolation changed into consolation and missionary zeal: 'did not hearts burn within us?' (Lk 24: 32).

The major challenges facing the Irish Church are surely those around the crisis of faith at a time of secularisation, and moving to what Pope Francis has called his dream of 'a poor Church for the poor'. However, I have argued here that more immediate obstacles need also to be addressed, namely those around sexuality and gender in particular. And I have proposed that an open listening to the 'sense of faith' of the faithful around these issues can be first steps toward the necessary removal of these obstacles.

In the end, and already along the way, the two disciples experienced a renewal of hope, of energy, of joy. Do we want to undergo a similar experience? Let's begin walking!

Questions

- *The Irish Catholic Bishops stated that 'synods are not instruments to change Church teaching but rather to help to apply it more pastorally.' Pope Francis, in Let us Dream, says that 'tradition is not a museum, teaching changes and doctrine is not static but grows and develops.' What do these two statements have to offer as we embark on this synodal process?*

- *What circumstances might ensure that those participating in the synodal process would have 'parrhesia' around issues such as sexuality and women in the church?*

The Practice of Synodality

8

A SYNOD OR AN ASSEMBLY? THAT IS THE QUESTION

Eugene Duffy

Eugene Duffy is a priest of the diocese of Achonry where he serves as Episcopal Vicar for Pastoral Renewal. In this chapter he outlines the development of diocesan synods and situates Pope Francis's call for a synodal Church within the context of previous post-conciliar efforts at renewal at diocesan level in Ireland. He shows that there has been a pattern of initial enthusiasm for efforts at renewal and restructuring but also of a failure in many instances to follow through in taking the difficult decisions needed to effect real change.

Until his recent retirement, Dr Duffy was a fulltime member of staff of the Department of Theology & Religious Studies at Mary Immaculate College – University of Limerick – where he co-ordinated post graduate programmes in Christian Leadership in Education. Previously, he was Director of the Western Theological Institute and served on the staff of All Hallows College Dublin. He is a member of 'The Peter and Paul Seminar', an international group of ecclesiologists, canon lawyers and ecumenists researching and advocating for greater accountability and a conversion of institutional mentality within the Catholic Church.

Pope Francis has encouraged the development of a synodal Church since the beginning of his pontificate. While, much focus has been on both the synod of bishops and its agenda for the Synod of 2023, episcopal conferences have been encouraged to promote synodality in each of their respective areas, but the agenda really has to extend down to each diocese and each parish. This essay will look at the question of synodality in the context of a diocese and exploring the development of diocesan synods, and then reviewing various approaches to synodality that have occurred in Ireland since Vatican II.

The Development of Diocesan Synods

The practice of holding synods at a diocesan level has deep roots in the history of the Church.[148] The first documented diocesan synod, in the sense of establishing legislation or issuing disciplinary decrees, was held in Auxerre in 585. Documents regarding the diocesan synods that were held in the sixth century indicate that for the most part they were concerned with the transmission of the decisions of provincial councils. They were means of keeping presbyters informed of ecclesial developments and of maintaining discipline. The situation remained the same through to the tenth century. Although there are frequent references to these synods very few of their acts or decrees have survived. By the time of the Gregorian Reform (mid-eleventh – early twelfth centuries), the synodal structure was one of the main ways that this papal reform was implemented across Europe. So for example, the synods of Kells, Rathbreasil and Cashel, which established the diocesan boundaries in Ireland, were instances of that reform process.

The first time that diocesan synods are mandated is at Lateran IV (1215). In this context, it is quite clear that the reforms of the Council itself are to be transmitted to the whole Church through provincial

---

148 For a useful outline of the development of diocesan synods see. O. Pontal, 'Évolution historique du synode diocésain', in *L'Anne canonique, hors série*, Actes du VIIe congrès international de Droit Canonique, Paris (1992), Vol II, 521-536; a more detailed discussion of current synodal practices is to be found in Joseph Galea-Curmi, *The Diocesan Synod as a Pastoral Event: A Study of the Post-Conciliar Understanding of the Diocesan Synod*, Roma: Pontificia Universita Lateranense, 2005.

synods and their decrees in turn promulgated through diocesan synods. The provincial councils are to 'recite the canonical rules, especially those which have been laid down by this general council, so as to secure their observance, inflicting on transgressors the punishment due'.[149] Then each bishop is to hold a synod annually in his diocese: 'Whoever neglects to carry out this salutary statute is to be suspended from his benefices and from the execution of his office, until his superior decides to release him.'[150] Following Lateran IV there was a flourishing of diocesan synods throughout the thirteenth and fourteenth centuries. A significant development occurred in 1374 when Pope Gregory XI proposed that synods discuss the problems and issues arising in the local churches and not just confine themselves to promulgating the decrees of superior councils. Now diocesan synods could bring matters to the provincial council for their attention and not just act as the conduits for those above them. At the Council of Basel (Session 15, 1433), a very detailed instruction was set out for the convocation of an annual diocesan synod, with a view to providing clear instruction on the word of God, exhortation to good behaviour and the observance of one's duties, and the maintenance of good behaviour among the clergy.[151] Trent reiterated the obligation to hold diocesan synods annually with a view to maintaining ecclesiastical discipline, settling disputes and implementing the reforms of the Council itself.[152] Following Trent, reform-minded bishops were diligent in implementing the reforms of the Council by means of diocesan synods. Two notable examples were Charles Boromeo in Milan and Francis de Sales in Geneva.

In the latter part of the seventeenth century and throughout the eighteenth century, there was a decline in diocesan synodal activity. This was due to the aloofness of the bishops, the ineffectiveness of

149 Fourth Lateran Council, 1215, *Constitutions, no. 6, in Norman Tanner, ed., Decrees of the Ecumenical Councils, Vol I, (London: Sheed & Ward and Georgetown University Press, 1990), 236.*
150 Ibid.
151 Ibid., 473.
152 Council of Trent, Session 24, *Decree on Reform, Can 2, in Norman Tanner, ed., Decrees of the Ecumenical Councils, Vol II, 761.*

the synodal processes and interference by the secular powers. It was during this period that Pope Benedict XIV wrote his thirteen-volume work, *De Synodo diocesana*. Towards the end of the eighteenth century, attempts were made to make the diocesan synod more democratic in its decision-making processes. Tensions persisted about the respective rights of the bishop and his clergy in confirming the decrees of these synods. The ill-fated Synod of Pistoia in 1786 demonstrates how a diocesan synod, despite the agreement of bishop and clergy, could act in a fashion at variance with the wider Church. Its decrees were condemned by a subsequent 'national' synod of the Tuscan bishops in 1787 and eventually by the Pope in 1794. It serves as an example of the problems that can arise even in a properly constituted diocesan synod. Thus, it can be seen that internal and external factors diminished the enthusiasm for diocesan synods until well into the nineteenth century. Vatican I intended to discuss their importance, particularly because annual diocesan synods were not being held regularly. The Council's preparatory documents indicate that the proposal was to mandate diocesan synods to be held every three years. However, due to the premature conclusion to the Council the matter was not decided.

The 1917 Code of Canon Law (CC 356-362) legislated significantly for diocesan synods, mandating that they be held every ten years to deal with those things necessary and useful for the clergy of the diocese. Interestingly, no censures were to be applied to bishops who failed to convoke a synod, indicating the lessons that had been learned over previous centuries. While the synods envisaged by the Code did not exclude the laity participating, they were essentially clerical affairs. Despite the legislation of 1917 diocesan synods remained relatively infrequent and in so far as they were deployed, it was to apply universal law within a diocese.

When John XXIII announced the summoning of an ecumenical council in 1959, he simultaneously announced the summoning of a diocesan synod for the diocese of Rome. Obviously, the Pope wanted to show that the renewal of the Church and the renewal of the diocese of Rome were all of a piece. Yet, the contrast between the two could not be more stark. The Roman synod was a disappointment, since it was a clerical gathering and juridical in nature, following the lines of the prevailing ecclesiology and the existing Code. It was then completely superseded by the reforms of Vatican II.

Vatican II as a Basis for Diocesan Synods

The question of diocesan synods did not figure significantly in the work of Vatican II. A number of recommendations had been made to the Preparatory Commission regarding the holding of diocesan synods and in one of the early drafts of the document on the Missions the topic was included but later dropped, as it was felt it belonged more to the work of the Commission for the Revision of the Code of Canon Law. It has been convincingly argued by Joseph Galea-Curmi that there is no reference to diocesan synods in Vatican II, despite the fact that the use of the word 'synods' in *Christus Dominus no. 36* is often interpreted as referring to diocesan synods. He shows that this term refers to synods in the context of the communion ecclesiarum, not to synodal activity in the particular Churches.[153]

The question may be asked then: if the Council did not speak explicitly about diocesan synods, on what basis may its work be seen to support their revitalisation? The entire ecclesiology of Vatican II represents a complete reformulation of how the Church understands itself. Rather than starting with its hierarchical constitution, the *Dogmatic Constitution* on the Church began with the People of God, stressing the equality of all members of the Church on the basis of their baptism which gives them a share in Christ's priestly, prophetic and kingly offices (LG 9 - 17). They are a pilgrim people, 'as they journey through temptations and tribulations', in other words, a synodal people as they make their way towards the fullness of the Kingdom of God. While the primacy of the Pope is clearly upheld, his office is located within the context of the entire college of bishops. Each bishop in his diocese is then described as a Vicar of Christ and they 'are not to be regarded as a vicars of the Roman Pontiff' (LG 27), marking a reversal of the understanding of their

---

153 *The Diocesan Synod as a Pastoral Event*, 22-37.

governance roles that was widely accepted up to the time of the Council. The collegial nature of the episcopate was presented as a balance to the excess of emphasis on papal primacy that had obtained since the end of the nineteenth century. Therefore, greater responsibility is devolved to the individual bishops in their dioceses, as can be seen in numerous conciliar documents. The bishop in turn is to listen to his subjects, to promote their welfare and invite their collaboration with him in his ministry. Thus, a much flatter organisational structure is envisaged, with greater participation in all levels of governance. This can be seen in the institution of the Synod of Bishops by Pope Paul VI during the Council, the range of responsibilities being entrusted to the episcopal conferences, as well as the promotion of presbyteral and pastoral councils at diocesan level.

The Council itself was a meeting of the global Church, with a representation of cultures and traditions not previously experienced on such a grand scale. The experience of the conciliar bishops in encountering such a richness of diversity in the Church liberated them to appreciate the importance of local customs and traditions. It facilitated the recognition of the need to accommodate ecclesial structures and methodologies to this global diversity, as can be seen in the recommendation to implant the gospel with sensitivity to 'the particular social and cultural conditions' of those with whom it works. The importance of inculturating the Gospel took on a new impetus as can be seen in the Constitution on the Sacred Liturgy, (SC 37-40) when it states that: 'even in the liturgy the Church does not wish to impose a rigid uniformity in matters which do not involve the faith or the good of the whole community. Rather does she respect and foster the qualities and talents of the various races and nations' (SC 37). Similarly, in the Pastoral Constitution on the Church in the Modern World, the Council stated: 'This adaptation in preaching the revealed word should remain the law of evangelisation. In this way, in every nation, the capacity to express Christ's message in its own fashion is stimulated and at the same time a fruitful interchange is encouraged between the Church and various cultures' (GS 44). As Ormond Rush has noted, commenting on this article, 'God is at work revealing and saving already within local cultures, and the Church is here being called to discern God's presence and to learn from it'.[154]

As well as recognising what whole cultures can offer to the life of the Church, the Council also affirmed the contribution of each individual baptised member of the Church. Every human person has a contribution to make to the life of the Church, since all are created in the image and likeness of God. The baptised are uniquely gifted by the Holy Spirit, leading them to hear and recognise God's voice addressing them and then enabling them to respond. This gift of hearing and responding to God's word is situated within a community context; the believer never exists in isolation but as part of a believing community. The Council affirms in very clear language the value of the insights of the faithful in the Church:

> The universal body of the faithful who have received the anointing of the holy one, (see 1 Jn 2, 20 and 27), cannot be mistaken in belief. It displays this particular quality through a supernatural sense of the faith in which the whole people when "from the bishops to the last of the faithful laity", it expresses the consent of all in matters of faith and morals. Through this sense of the faith which is aroused and sustained by the Spirit of truth, the People of God, under the guidance of the sacred magisterium to which it is faithfully obedient, receive no longer the words of human beings but truly the word of God (see 1 Th 2, 13); it adheres indefectibly to the 'faith which was once for all delivered to the saints' (Ju 3); it penetrates more deeply into that same faith through right judgement and applies it more fully to life (LG 12).

Post Vatican II Synodality in Ireland

Since the Council, synodality has found many expressions in the life of the local Church, apart from the formal convocation of a diocesan synod. These can include the diocesan presbyteral council, the

---

154 *The Vison of Vatican II: Its Fundamental Principles, (Collegeville, MN: The Liturgical Press, 2019), 227.*

diocesan pastoral council and finance council, a range of diocesan commissions dealing with liturgy, education, youth ministry, family ministry, etc., as well as various councils or groups that meet at parish level to address a variety of pastoral issues. Limerick is the only Irish diocese to have had a diocesan synod since Vatican II. However, various convocations of clergy or of clergy and laity have taken place in most Irish dioceses with a view to exploring ways to renew the life of faith in the local Church. The first of those convocations occurred in the 1980s and were generally of clergy only. Yet, despite their almost exclusively clerical membership, they produced significant and useful pastoral plans for their respective dioceses. For example, the diocese of Armagh held its 'assembly of priests' in September 1981, which did include religious sisters engaged in pastoral work in the diocese. The assembly, in the words of one of its members, 'was a serious attempt to reflect on our priesthood, to honestly analyse whether the way we do our work could be improved, to identify important areas of pastoral concern that would require extra attention over the next few years and to plan accordingly'.[155] While the assembly made laudable recommendations about the renewal of the lives of the priests, spiritually, intellectually, pastorally and socially, it also addressed the wider issue of the nature and scope of pastoral action in the diocese. The plans drawn up were impressive by any standards, which included:

> missionary work "especially in view of our present diocesan shortage of priests" in a third world territory; the establishment of two Action for Justice groups, one North and one South of the border; to highlight the injustices behind the Northern troubles as well as problems of industrial relations, unemployment and social deprivation ... a diocesan Resource Centre of Information and Communication with a trained media utilization team ... seek out the lapsed and provide for the spiritual and educational needs of youth and adult ... to create liturgy which expresses the faith of a living and caring community,

---

155 Gerard McGinnity, 'Armagh Diocesan Assembly of Priests', *The Furrow* 32 (1981), 750.

gathered to celebrate actively and in a way that has relevance and meaning for us, our belief in the Risen Christ, constantly calling us to reconciliation, service, justice and truth.[156]

A sample of the final documents from other dioceses show a similarly creative and energetic agenda being set for the renewal of ecclesial life. For example, from the Achonry Assembly of Priests meeting in 1983, there were detailed recommendations for the support of priests' spirituality, better cooperation among priests across neighbouring parishes; efforts were to be made to establish community care councils in groups of parishes; to work with local communities in organising seminars to support local development and co-operation; the establishment of a parish council and also a properly equipped liturgy team in each parish; more work to be done on pre-sacramental preparation for all sacraments; to put in place adult education programmes; that a foreign mission from the diocese be considered. The priests of the diocese of Killaloe held their assembly in 1984 and similarly addressed issues of priestly ministry, adult education, pre-sacramental preparation, youth ministry and the problems of unemployment.

The Berger Method, as it was called, was the process used in the Armagh and indeed most of the diocesan assemblies that took place in the 1980s. It involved naming the issues that needed to be addressed, analysing them and then creatively imagining a future better than the past or current situation. The naming of the current realities often proved a painful experience for those in various leadership roles, and it is hard to avoid the impression that some of those critical analyses impacted negatively on the bishops involved and most likely on all of them. Despite those negative aspects of the process, the imaging of the future, as expressed rather typically in the Armagh, Achonry and Killaloe assemblies, was positive and commendable for its vision and practicality. The fact is, however, that very little of the vision was ever systematically followed through in practice and similar visions for renewal continue to be articulated up to the present.

156 Ibid. 753-754.

Over the past decade or so, another round of diocesan assemblies has been taking place. These more recent assemblies have included all the members of the People of God in a diocese, not just the clergy. The formats that these have taken and the processes used have varied considerably. Many of them have been labelled as a 'listening process' with a view to providing a basis for a diocesan pastoral plan. In 2012 the diocese of Killaloe conducted an extensive listening process, as well as two online surveys. The data from these were processed by a Steering Committee established by the Diocesan Pastoral Council and a theological reflection group. The result was a diocesan pastoral plan, with ten strands, to run from 2013 to 2020. The ten strands included: leadership; partnership in ministry; liturgy; spirituality and prayer; youth ministry; adult faith education; justice, peace and the integrity of creation; diocesan safeguarding services; communications; management of resources.[157] Although the social, economic and religious landscape in Ireland had changed greatly since the 1980s the issues being addressed were remarkably similar to those identified then. The issues raised in Killaloe in the second decade of this century are echoed in other dioceses that have undertaken similar processes.[158]

In a way similar to other Irish dioceses, the largest diocese in the country, Dublin, held assemblies of priests in 1981 and 1983. A wider consultation with the people of the diocese was undertaken in 1986 by the Pastoral Development and Renewal team. The recommendations from this included: training for lay ministry; adult faith formation; renewal of priests; greater involvement of young

157 *Builders of Hope: Pastoral Plan, Diocese of Killaloe, 2013-2020.* This replaced an earlier *Pastoral Plan 2004*, which had also involved a widespread consultative process, and which was originally proposed by a diocesan assembly of priests in 2002. The issues in *Pastoral Plan 2004* are quite similar to those in the later plan.

158 The Diocese of Killala held a listening process in 2017-2018, which has formed the basis of its pastoral plan https://www.killaladiocese.org/assembly/); more recently a task force in the diocese of Dublin conducted a listening process with a view to advising the Archbishop in his pastoral planning, and similar issues to those already mentioned were identified (https://dublindiocese.ie/wp-content/uploads/2021/11/Building-Hope-Task-Force-Report.pdf). Other diocesan assemblies are mentioned in other essays in this volume.

people; wider and ongoing consultation structures; and a pastoral policy including leadership and guidelines for lay ministry. Then in 2001 the Council of Priests recommended to Cardinal Connell that a diocesan synod should be held. A new council of priests made a similar recommendation the following year. This was supported by 90% of the priests of the diocese and 93% of the laity, following a wide consultative process. The hope was 'that synod, unlike other church assemblies, will be a participative and collaborative way of episcopal governance, producing binding decrees and putting in place executive structures and resources to ensure that it has pastoral results rather than just producing documents'.[159] Despite the overwhelming support for the diocesan synod, Cardinal Connell opted not to proceed at that point in view of his imminent retirement and left the option open for his successor to proceed with it. However, Archbishop Martin did not consider the time opportune to do so and so the project was abandoned.

The most high profile synodal process undertaken in Ireland in recent times has been the Limerick Diocesan Synod, the first to be held in Ireland for eighty years. The reasons given for the convocation of the synod were: i) gratitude for the inheritance of faith in the diocese; ii) to digest the teachings of Vatican II; iii) to come to grips with the social and cultural changes impacting on people's lives; iv) to address the current, challenging ecclesial realities, v) to respond to the invitation of Pope Francis for pastoral and missionary conversion.

The synodal process was determined by a twenty-four member Preparatory Commission in line with the canonical legislation for synodal gatherings. The Commission worked on the recruitment of 400 delegates who would be representative of the people of the diocese in all their different conditions. The synodal process began with an eighteen month period of consultation and listening not just in parishes but in a wide variety of pastoral contexts, including third level colleges, the Travelling Community, various ethnic and language groups, as well those involved in business, arts and sport. A

---

159 Gerry Tanham, 'Issues facing the Diocese', *Link-Up* 27 (2002), 9. The issue is devoted almost entirely to the proposed synod.

more detailed outline of the entire process is provided in the essay by Eamonn Fitzgibbon, elsewhere in this volume.[160]

The Limerick Synod was a most comprehensive effort in terms of preparation, the integrity of the processes involved, the representative nature of the delegates, the range of issues that was presented for discussion and ultimately for voting. It is obvious, too, that it was a very costly undertaking, given the professionalism with which the whole process was conducted. One hundred proposals were eventually voted on, of which 97 were approved. These then formed the basis of the diocesan plan for the following ten years: 'Moving Forward Together in Hope'. The plan eventually focused on six themes: i) community and sense of belonging; ii) pastoral care of the family; iii) young people; iv) liturgy and life; v) faith formation and education; vi) new models of leadership. Again, the themes are not dissimilar to those that have been emerging in other dioceses over the past forty years. The Limerick plan is detailed in terms of the way the stages for implementation are set out. The fact that the resolutions of the Synod have a canonically binding force gives the plan greater weight than the less formal assemblies and listening processes that have been held elsewhere in Ireland. The real test of the Synod's success is in the implementation. The Limerick diocesan website provides a 'progress report' for the following year, but nothing since then. Obviously, the pandemic has impacted progress, but the questions may legitimately be posed: did the enormous effort expended and expenses incurred prove more fruitful than the less formal and less costly processes elsewhere? Did the process itself generate a greater commitment on the part of the faithful in the diocese, including the clergy, to a genuine renewal of faith and practice? Have the obstacles that inhibited the efforts at renewal forty years ago been addressed and removed? Did the force of canonically binding resolutions eventually strengthen the Bishop's ability to affect the desired renewal? Is there a sufficiently robust evaluation process in place to identify progress being made and the identification of the blockages that occur? Is there a strategy in

160 The full details of all of the synodal process are available on the Limerick diocesan website: www.synod2016.com. This is a most comprehensive resource. An account of this synod is also to be found in E. Fitzgibbons' essay in this volume.

place to address the blockages once they have been identified? While some of these questions are specific to the Limerick synodal process, they are questions that will have to be faced by all of those who are engaging in any form of synodal process.

The outcome of all of the post-conciliar assemblies and synod seem to be very similar. There is no shortage of ideas and idealism, but there seems to be a dearth of commitment to following through on the proposals. It is a real cause for concern that the same issues have been presented for about forty years, and little of any great significance has been done to move the agendas forward and to deliver concrete pastoral actions that would respond to the needs which were identified. This surely raises questions about the accountability of leadership in dioceses. Despite the urgency of the needs identified there appears to have been a lack of enthusiasm or energy to implement most of the plans that were formulated. Perhaps at times, the plans were overly ambitious and issues within those plans were not ranked in order of priority, with the result that the urgent and less urgent were all looked upon as too great an undertaking with which to engage. Another very serious shortcoming is that is also a great lack of evaluation of all of these undertakings. There is very little empirical evidence to show what was or was not achieved on the basis of the various plans adopted. This leads to further problems as subsequent efforts at planning and renewal are put in place. Nobody rightly knows what has succeeded or not and why that may be the case. This generates another obstacle for the next attempts at renewal because the more often people are invited to participate in these exercises that don't yield the expected outcomes the more dissatisfied and alienated they will become. There is an incremental depletion of energy the more often people move through the stages of planning processes that are not brought to a conclusion and not properly evaluated. Perhaps the time has come to explore what it is that is blocking our lack of delivery when it comes to ecclesial renewal in Ireland. Until such a task is undertaken, it seems to matter little whether the process followed is a formal diocesan synod or simply an assembly of the people of the diocese. Indeed if a proper culture of accountability were in place a diocesan assembly, like many of those that have already taken place, may be just as effective pastorally as a formal synod.

Questions

- *History paints a bleak picture of the implementation and outcomes of synods and synod-like processes. How can we, as the People of God, ensure that history is not repeated as we embark on a new synodal journey?*

- *The Dogmatic Constitution on the Church (Vatican II) provided the basis for 'the Bishop to listen to his subjects, to promote their welfare and invite their collaboration with him in his ministry'. Is this reflected in the Irish Church today, sixty years later? Are we hopeful that the current synodal process will create the circumstances whereby Vatican II can be fully realised?*

9

ON A LEVEL PLAYING FIELD? THE GERMAN SYNODAL EXPERIMENT

Bernd Hagenkord SJ
(trans. Eamonn Conway)

Bernd Hagenkord, a German Jesuit priest (1968 – 2021), was appointed as one of two spiritual guides to the Synodaler Weg, The two-year synodal process begun by the German Bishops in association with the laity in 2019. The German Synodal Way was triggered by the findings of a report that looked into sexual abuse within the Church and seeks to address a wide range of questions on authority, structure and faith. This chapter outlines the approach taken by the German bishops and presents an account of the challenges encountered so far.

Prior to 2019, Fr Hagenkord headed the German-language section of Vatican Radio and participated in many of the recent World Synods of Bishops held in Rome. Previously he had spent many years in youth chaplaincy. He died on 23 July 2021 following a long illness.

It all began with us staring into the abyss. After a decade of having to deal with sexual violence in the church, the so-called MHG study was published in 2018[161] and in response to its findings the Church commissioned a five-year period of investigation into the topic of sexual abuse by priests, deacons and male religious in Germany. A long list of crimes and failures emerged, as well as an insight into the systemic causes that had enabled abuse and cover-up. The bishops and the representatives of the laity in the Church came to the conclusion that the problems of the Church must now be investigated in full.

That was the opening shot for what the Church in Germany has been undertaking as the "Synodal Way" since 2019, a very broad debate on many topics without any predetermined outcomes. Of course no one is under the illusion that everything will be fine again afterwards. The debate about abuse in the Church has led to massive formal resignations from the Church faithful as well several expressions of deep-seated frustration. Even the most loyal of the faithful are leaving the Church because they see too many contradictions in it to the message of Jesus. It would be an illusion to think that a synodal process could rectify all this but at least it can seek to remove the obstacles that stand in the way of the proclamation of the Gospel.

Since the beginning of his pontificate, Pope Francis has emphasised that the Church must once again become an evangelising Church. This same message he gave in a letter to the Church in Germany in the summer of 2019 at the beginning of the Synodal Way.[162] For the sake of proclaiming the Gospel we must speak about what are at times deeply-rooted problems that stand in the way. In this letter the Pope speaks of a 'change of epoch' that both 'justifies and necessitates' engagement with questions both new and ancient. In the original text here by Pope Francis there is a play on words: we are living through not just an epoch of change but a change of epoch. That reflects well the drama of the situation.

---

161 This was an inter-disciplinary research project undertaken into sexual violence in the Roman Catholic Church in Germany by experts based in Mannheim, Heidelberg and Giessßen (MHG) from 2014-2018.

162 http://www.vatican.va/content/francesco/de/letters/2019/documents/papa-francesco_20190629_lettera-fedeligermania.html.

What is the "Synodal Way"?

The Synodal Way is a 'successful model', as the President of the Central Committee of German Catholics (the official lay committee), Prof. Thomas Sternberg, put it in April 2021. The question arises as to what exactly this model is. For, strictly speaking, there is no canonical form for a 'Synodal Way' in the Church.

The synodal assembly is at the centre of the synodal path. Its 230 members include all bishops, as well as representatives of all Church groups: lay people, priests, those in pastoral ministries, religious orders and communities, theologians. The life of the Church is intended to be represented as broadly as possible.

However, the assembly is not a parliament; as with a synod, it is also advisory in nature. The implementation of resolutions lies with the bishops in their dioceses. This ensures compliance with canonical regulations as well as unity with the world Church.

The plan was to work for two years, with four plenary assemblies and meetings of working groups in between. Covid-19 thwarted all of this and so digital meetings not originally provided for in the statutes had to be inserted, and this has led to the whole process being extended by at least a year. The flexible format of the process has proven to be useful here as it enabled new formats and processes to be tried out. The process lends itself to adaptation.

But as already indicated: canon law does not recognize this way of proceeding, nor, for example, does the 'Synodal Way' meet the requirements of a synod in a particular Church. Canonically, the Synodal Way is therefore a *nullum*, that is, has no standing in canon law and does not follow any clear guidelines. The decision to proceed in this way was consciously taken. The bishops and the laity wanted an approach that was deliberately being kept open-ended. The disadvantage of this was, and is, that every single step has to be negotiated anew. The Synodal Way cannot rely on canonical specifications and when concluded cannot claim canonical validity. The advantage is that this approach can respond to the issues of the day. The contents do not have to be based upon formal requirements and also do not have to be clarified in advance in terms of how they accord with canon law. That makes the process flexible and adaptable. In addition, it offers more scope for what's new and for developments than a defined format would be able to permit.

A special feature is that all participants have equal rights in the debates. The seating arrangement underlines this: participants sit alphabetically and are not separated according to whether they are bishops, priests or lay people. Requests to speak are made by raising one's hand, everyone is treated equally, and there is no hierarchy in the course of the debate. However, that all highlights the structural challenge: in order to enable participants to speak and vote freely and openly about everything in the Church, the Synodal Way has given itself a structure that is located outside of the relevant canonical provisions. At the end of the day it is not a synod. The price for this is that this process cannot produce anything that is binding. So, on the one hand, we have a gathering that allows for free, open debate, and at times disagreement. On the other, the question remains as to how resolutions passed can be incorporated into the Church's canonical structures.

A form of synodality

From the beginning, the one great question facing the 'Synodal Way' was that of the binding nature of its decisions. The committee works in an advisory capacity, but at the same time when outlining its responsibilities the bishops had set out from the beginning that the decisions arrived at should be 'binding'. So, on the one hand, there are complex voting methods and procedures, and, on the other hand, the final decision, as already indicated, remains with the bishops.

What looks from the outside like a contradiction feels in practice like the emergence of new forms of synodality. The Church is undergoing transformation and requires new forms of authority and unity. Those who lead and those who advise must find a new way of relating to one another. Diversity and unity in the Church have to be recalibrated. These are all formulations that point to a central theme that now preoccupies the Church worldwide and also the Pope: synodality. The Synodal Way sees itself here as an experiment.

In his letter to the Synodal Way, the Pope spoke out clearly against mistaking a synod for a parliament; he particularly does not want authority to reside with a collective body. Instead, there needs to be a path leading to spiritual discernment, a spiritual path. This will have to be considered in more detail below but here we should already point out that the Synodal Way differs significantly in this respect from the culture of debate, for example, one finds in the synods of the churches of the Reformation.

Above all, what the Synodal Way has achieved in its meetings so far is a new culture in regard to how matters are discussed. Equality in the course of the debate, for example, is not there to disguise the prevailing hierarchies in the Church and so to pretend that everyone is equal. However, it ensures that a new, at times argumentative form of debate is now extant in the Church.

Generally, members of the group do not tend to know each other and we in the Catholic Church do not have much experience with synodal structures or democratic processes. All of this only develops slowly in the course of the process. This definitely includes a healthy conflict culture. It is no secret that people hold differing convictions regarding core issues of faith and discipline. But now they find themselves together in one room and are obliged to talk to each other instead of just about each other. In such circumstances our Church matures and synodality happens.

Criticism

One of the most visible features of the Synodal Way is the sometimes massive criticism that is unleashed against it. Initially, this has been from within the Church in Germany, but it is now becoming increasingly shrill from outside as well. In media circles that call themselves Catholic, we hear 'apostasy' and 'heresy' bandied about thoughtlessly and without any proper understanding of what these concepts mean. Even fans of synodality see the German endeavour as a particular path leading away from Rome or at least one separating local churches from one another.

The basis for this fundamental criticism is the understanding of authority. Groups that presuppose allegedly never-changing Church teaching and consider the Church's social form to be characterised above all by hierarchy and obedience also consider their inner-ecclesial dominance to be endangered by synodal processes. The Synodal Way is not the only target for criticism here; Pope Francis also has had to face alleged *dubia,* that is, a formal doubt expressed by some cardinals, concerning his doctrinal statements. Ultimately, this was nothing more than a questioning of his authority. The particular ecclesial structure of the Church in Germany, which is characterised by a strong sense of independence when it comes to theology and the role of the laity, leaves the Synodal Way particularly attractive when it comes to fundamental criticism.

The critics overlook or do not want to recognise that reform of the Church aimed at restoration is no longer possible. The research mentioned at the beginning of this chapter as well as many other studies have shown that it is not enough to reform poor forms of structures that in and of themselves may be good. The structure in and of itself contributes to abuse and also to dwindling trust in the Church and thus also in its message. That is why the issues must be pursued in such a fundamental way.

What the critics also overlook or do not want to acknowledge is the fact that there have been very different and contradicting convictions on certain matters in the Church for quite a long time. The Church has long been stretched to breaking point on some issues. The Synodal Way is now a good opportunity for people with different positions to come together, hear one another, question one another critically and dispute with one another.

A break-up would mean people saying goodbye to each other and going their own way. The Synodal Way, however, brings together people who invest great passion in the Church, which they love. This cannot be denied of anyone who is participating! Reservations, questions, reproaches and wounds need to be acknowledged so that you can even begin a conversation. We cannot pretend that these deep, contradictory positions and disputes do not exist just because they have too often been hidden or have only covertly entered into conversation on a smaller scale.

The Synodal Way does not create these disputes and contradictory positions; it only renders them visible. And more importantly, these different points of view are put together in one room, so to speak, and get to talk to one another not about one another.

Of course, this does not suit those who claim sovereignty over how others interpret the Church and faith and would much rather determine it for them themselves.

Understood in this way, the Synodal Way touches a sore point that goes way beyond Germany. The fact that the German form of synodality has also been criticised in Asia and the USA, and that heavy weapons like 'schism' and 'heresy' have been deployed, show that the problems Germany is facing exist outside Germany as well.

Strengths and weaknesses

The fact that there is a lot of fundamental and ultimately destructive criticism of the Synodal Way which must be clearly countered does not mean that there are not also problems and weaknesses in the process. It would be negligent not to face up to this.

The greatest weakness results from the structure: precisely because the process is open and flexible, it is not yet possible to foresee what the outcomes will be. Not even the shape of the outcomes is foreseeable, because some matters can certainly only be decided on a global Church level, matters that are clearly urgent and pressing. But there is also a lot of controversy on local issues, so it is by no means definite that at the end of the process there will be outcomes which everyone, or even most participants, will be able to unite behind.

This is a risk that the Synodal Way is aware of and recognises as a vulnerability. In addition, there are other concerns, or to put it in the language of the Pope, there are temptations. Francis makes this very clear in the letter he issued at the commencement of the Synodal Way already referred to. The first temptation, for example, is to see reform exclusively in structural terms, 'to believe that the solutions to current and future problems can only be achieved by reforming structures, organizations and administration'. This might bring about a 'modernized ecclesiastical organism' but would lack the soul of the Gospel. Without succumbing to national stereotypes one can see a very German-like temptation here. The Church in Germany has a strong and domineering structure, underpinned by a lot of money and many Church employees in pastoral care and administration. To see the solution only in these terms will not bring about a solution.

The second temptation is related to the first. Here, too, I can cite the Pope: 'Whenever an ecclesiastical community tried to get out of its problems on its own, and only trusted in its own strength, its own methods and its own intelligence, it only ever ended in increasing and sustaining the evil it set out to overcome.' Above all, the reality that we belong to a worldwide Church seems to prevent easy local solutions. Here the Pope rightly warns that solutions will never come from relying solely upon one's own strengths. Synodality always has to do with thinking outside the box; this is a specifically Catholic insight.

Over against these weaknesses, or, as the Pope would say, temptations, there is one great strength that goes a long way towards outweighing them. And this strength lies in a new, open and flexible form of internal Church dialogue. Even if it is difficult to put up with the many clearly diverging perspectives and convictions and to bring them together, this is where the actual core of synodality is to be found. Pope Paul VI had already formulated the basis for this in his first encyclical, *Ecclesiam Suam:*

> It becomes obvious in a dialogue that there are various ways of coming to the light of faith and it is possible to make them all converge on the same goal. However divergent these ways may be, they can often serve to complete each other. They encourage us to think on different lines. They force us to go more deeply into the subject of our investigations and to find better ways of expressing ourselves. It will be a slow process of thought, but it will result in the discovery of elements of truth in the opinion of others and make us want to express our teaching with great fairness.

What Pope Paul VI has to say here about dialogue in general applies particularly to dialogue within the Church. And the real strength of the Synodal Way is to make progress in regard to this.

What has happened so far

When the Synodal Way began, four subject areas were identified that were to be debated in separate forums. One related to authority and how it is regulated in the Church, another to the role of women, yet another was to address forms of priestly ministry, and the final one, the proclamation of the Church's teaching on sexuality.

These topics were not randomly selected. They bring a focus to bear upon debates that have existed for a long time and which address fundamental problems. Together they represent several key questions and areas of conflict. And it is good that these topics are being debated; this alone makes the Synodal Way worthwhile.

How exactly these are approached and what comes out of them cannot be reported here as the debates are ongoing. It can be noted, however, that the topic that triggered these debates, namely sexual violence and abuse, is also playing a major role in the debates on the Synodal Way. Victims and survivors of sexual violence in the Church are being invited to participate and to offer their perspectives. The Advisory Board for Affected Persons, which the Church in Germany established, has the right to attend as guests and to speak during the Synodal Way gatherings. Sexual abuse had so affected the Church that victims and survivors cannot be left out of the synodal deliberations. But given that the work of the Synodal Way is far from concluded, it is not yet apparent how the various perspectives will eventually be brought together.

A Spiritual Way

From the beginning, the Synodal Way was intended to be what secular, democratic processes for forming opinions are not: a spiritual way. Pope Francis also confirmed this in his letter: 'Without the Holy Spirit, without the centrality of proclamation of the Gospel, without bearing in mind the weak and marginalized, nothing happens. The answer to the crisis we face can only be found in this way.'

It is important to deal wisely with problems; statistics, analyses, forecasts and all of that are, of course, important. One can also in this way recognise the signs of the times. The Church should not stand still; however, there is more to being a believer than just this. A synodal approach should not try merely to reform or rescue the status quo, or merely to rescue the dwindling strength and significance of the Church in Germany. What matters is to distinguish spiritually where God wants to lead God's Church.

But just as with the question of the open nature of the Synodal Way, there are also several question marks here. What exactly does it mean to walk such a spiritual path together? And what, specifically, is its impact and outcomes?

One of the first hurdles was to get used to the routine: it was customary to pray before and after meetings and to celebrate Mass together, but something really important happened in between, i.e., the debate and the work on jointly formulated texts.

It is not uncommon for the term 'spiritual process' to be met with a certain mistrust. It is sometimes wrongfully assumed that to raise matters to a spiritual level is to play them down and render them harmless. However, the opposite is the case: when things get spiritual they become really serious because now God is in play.

It is and remains difficult to connect this spiritual dimension with the debates and discussions. Yet the spiritual reveals itself in very simple things: in respect and in listening and in basically acknowledging that behind the contributions of others is a fellow believer.

Unlike rules of procedure or rules of debate, however, the spiritual dimension cannot be determined by shared decision-making. Each and every one participating has to determine how that works for themselves. That is why spiritual accompaniment seems important to the process. Two people have been appointed to accompany the process, one of whom is the author of this article. Maria Boxberg and I have no voting rights and we do not get involved in the content of the debates, but we are something like the Spirit's advocates. We're not there to lead prayer, arrange the spiritual programme or to organise Mass. Rather, we assist in ensuring that the spiritual dimension permeates the entire process. And that too is a path, a map for which is not given in advance.

Above all else, to differentiate spiritually where God is leading God's Church is not to fall back on general principles or convictions.

Nor is it an exercise in applying general norms, whether human, Christian or ecclesial, to an individual case; it is not about the individual realisation of what is general. God's presence always stretches well beyond general norms.

It is about personal responsibility for one's own faith and for the transmission and preaching of faith to others. It is about distinguishing what is needed in terms of care; and prayer, over and over again. It is about nuances and inner freedom, and the action of God in my own life; it is about experiencing and perceiving. This is all the opposite of unambiguity. And so, this can be a source of fear because there are no automatic or quick-fix solutions to problems.

What it's about is that I take up my position in and entrust myself to the process freely and in right relationship to God, to Jesus Christ, and that I make decisions together with others with whom I share responsibility for these decisions, the outcomes of which are not yet foreseeable.

That is a demanding undertaking. It is a real struggle to actually accommodate this spiritual dimension. This is not meant to denigrate anyone's good will or their spirituality. However, the dynamics of the debate develop their own dynamics. This is why we have to learn anew and practise both incorporating the spiritual dimension and debating conflictual issues.

Finally, the spiritual dimension is itself just as important as the other points to be discussed. A spiritual awakening is needed in the Church, on the Synodal Way, and beyond. This awakening must face up to the problems in the Church and learn how to deal with them.

Much of what has happened so far already has spiritual elements and if these are cultivated it is an opportunity for such an awakening. The Synodal Way can remove obstacles along the path so that people can once again be drawn close to the Gospel and have it take root in their lives.

In its conflict and in its prayer, in its debate and spiritual discernment, the Synodal Way is the necessary and urgent first step leading to forms of communication, decision-making and structures for the Church in Germany that are more appropriate to the proclamation of the Gospel.

Questions

- *The synodal process in Ireland, similar to the Synodal Way in Germany, cannot produce any outcomes that are binding in canon law. To what extent might this impact on the level of engagement by participants, perhaps particularly by those who already have a lack of trust in the church?*

- *The German Synodal Way has adopted the practice of having two independent people to 'spiritually accompany' those involved in the process. What might the value of a similar concept be in the Irish process?*

10

A JOURNEY REMEMBERED - A JOURNEY CONTINUED

The Fifth Plenary Council of the Church in Australia

Timothy Costelloe SDB

Timothy Costelloe SDB, a Salesian of Don Bosco, is the Archbishop of Perth in Western Australia. He is the President of the Plenary Council, the Synodal process of the Australian Church, which has been underway since 2016. In this chapter he explains the origins of the decision of the bishops of Australia to convene a Plenary Council, highlighting the reasons for the bishops' conviction that this was a response to the call of the Holy Spirit. He also explains the bishops' determination that the Plenary Council be a Council for the whole Church, in which everyone's voice is important. Archbishop Costello details the various ways in which the Council facilitators have sought to engage the whole Catholic community in responding to the fundamental question of the Council: what is God asking of us in Australia at this time? He also refers to the challenges arising from the COVID-19 pandemic and the adjustments we are continuing to make in response to these challenges.

Prior to his appointment as a bishop, Archbishop Costello taught theology at the University of Notre Dame in Fremantle (Western Australia) and at the Catholic Theological College in Melbourne (Victoria). He holds a Licence in Systematic Theology from the Salesian Pontifical University in Rome, and a Doctorate in Theology from the Melbourne College of Divinity.

In May of 2016 Archbishop Mark Coleridge, Archbishop of Brisbane and President of the Australian Catholic Bishops' Conference, announced the decision of the bishops of Australia to convene a Plenary Council, the fifth in the history of the Catholic Church in Australia and the first since 1937. It will be only the third Plenary Council to be held by a Local Church since the Second Vatican Council. The other two were held in the Philippines in 1991 and in Poland in 1993.

The decision to hold a Plenary Council had been long in the making. Already, in the early years of the new millennium, the bishops had discerned the need for some kind of 'ecclesial event', which could bring the whole Church together with a view to evaluating our present situation and charting a course for the future. The need for such an event was clearly recognised. The idea that this event should take the form of a Plenary Council was much less clear.

Over a period of time, a consensus emerged among the bishops that the first step in discerning what the Spirit was asking of the Church in Australia must be some form of spiritual renewal. Gradually the decision to invite the whole Church to enter into a 'Year of Grace' was reached. It was to be a kind of national retreat, focused on the call of Pope John Paul II in his Apostolic Letter, *Novo Millennio Ineunte (NMI)*, to turn our eyes to the Lord. In the face of the many challenges being confronted by the Church in Australia the words of the pope offered us a clear direction:

The men and women of our own day — often perhaps uncon-sciously — ask believers not only to 'speak' of Christ, but in a cer-tain sense to 'show' him to them. And is it not the Church's task to reflect the light of Christ in every historical period, to make his face shine also before the generations of the new millennium? Our witness, however, would be hopelessly inadequate if we our-selves had not first *contemplated his face*. (NMI 16).

Before seeking solutions to the many issues facing the Catholic community in Australia we were invited, therefore, to turn our gaze to Christ, placing him at the centre of our individual and communal lives and at the heart of everything the Church was seeking to be and to do. Now in 2021 we are still harvesting the fruits of the Year of Grace, which began on Pentecost Sunday 2012 and concluded on Pentecost Sunday 2013.

Both during and after the Year of Grace the bishops continued to discern what further steps might be taken. Eventually the decision to convene a Plenary Council for the Church emerged. The formal deci-sion, taken at the plenary meeting of the Australian Catholic Bishops Conference in May 2016, was publicly announced shortly after and formally ratified by Pope Francis on 19 March, 2018.

Thus, a long process officially began; it is one which continues. Some significant decisions were quickly made. The first, and perhaps most far-reaching, was to structure the Plenary Council according to the two-fold structure of the Synod on the Family. Just as this Synod had two formal assemblies, the first in 2014 and the second in 2015, so the Plenary Council would have a first formal assembly in 2020 and a second in 2021. Because in the interim the crisis of the Covid-19 pandemic arose, and the decision was made to postpone the whole Council by a year. The first assembly, which was then held from October 3-10, 2021, has set the stage for the second assembly, which will take place in Sydney from July 4-9, 2022.

Because of the lock-downs in various parts of Australia in 2021, the first assembly was conducted in a 'multi-modal', online format rather than having all the participants in the Council gathering together in one venue as had been originally planned. This certainly added some complications to the planning process and forced us to modify both our structures and our expectations. We were, for example, faced with the challenge of conducting the Plenary Council across five different time-zones. We also had to radically re-think the liturgical and other prayer experiences which were essential to the creation of an atmosphere and mind-set conducive to discernment.

A second significant decision was to appoint a Facilitation Team whose task it would be to oversee the preparatory stage of the Council. This team is led by Ms Lana Turvey-Collins, who has been seconded from the formation team of Catholic Mission Australia. Lana is supported by a small group of people also seconded on a part-time basis from Catholic Mission, as well as a small number of others. To assist the Facilitation Team an Executive Committee was appointed, comprising fifteen people from around the country, the majority of them lay women and men. The planning of every aspect of the preparatory phase of the Plenary Council was entrusted to the Facilitation Team which was supported initially by the Executive Committee and is now supported by a number of newly-established groups, all working under the leadership of the Steering Committee, which has been responsible for the conduct of the first assembly and will continue to guide the work which has emerged from this assembly. Overseeing and collaborating with the work of all these people are the members of the Bishops Commission for the Plenary Council whose task it is to ensure that all the bishops are kept informed of developments.

At one of the early joint meetings of the Facilitation Team, the Executive Committee and the Bishops Commission, the fundamental question of the Plenary Council was formulated: 'what do you think God is asking of us in Australia at this time?' It is a deceptively simple question: it is also one which took us three days to clarify! Eventually, we moved from an initial phrasing of the question which asked people what they wanted the Plenary Council to achieve to one which asked people what, after a time of prayerful reflection, discussion and discernment, they had come to believe God might be asking of us. This invitation to go beyond our own particular hopes and dreams to a deeper reflection on God's 'dream' for the Church is a challenging one: it calls for humility, for openness to others, for a willingness to listen deeply and respectfully, and for a readiness to let go, if necessary, of some previously deeply held convictions or presuppositions. It calls, in other words, for a discerning heart.

With the wording of the question determined, the Facilitation Team and the Executive Committee together devised a process of national consultation, which had two distinct phases. The first was a process of *Listening and Dialogue* in which people were invited to enter into a time of genuine listening to each other. A methodology for this experience of listening and dialogue was offered and was taken up enthusiastically by many Catholics (and some others). The outcome of this process, conducted over a period of ten months, was that over 222,000 people took part in the listening and dialogue initiative. It was an impressive achievement and indicates how committed so many of our people have been, and continue to be, to this challenging, hope-filled journey.

All the submissions emerging from this national consultation were received by the National Centre for Pastoral Research (NCPR), an agency of the Australian Catholic Bishops Conference. Under the leadership of its director, Dr Trudy Dantis, these submissions were all carefully read and their contributions recorded. The results of this work led to a qualitative and quantitative analysis by the NCPR which was presented to the Facilitation Team, the Executive Committee and the Bishops' Commission over a three-day workshop. Approximately one hundred topics or items for consideration were identified. From these emerged six 'national themes for discernment', which were published as the basis for the next stage of the journey, a period of *Listening and Discernment*. To facilitate this process a method of spiritual conversation and contemplative discernment, based largely on Ignatian principles, was offered to the Catholic community.

The six themes emerging from the national consultation are all expressed as questions for reflection and all begin with these words: *What does it mean to be a Christ-centred Church which is ...?* Significantly, the idea of a 'Christ-centred Church' was originally identified as a seventh theme, but through engaging in a process of discernment the members of the Facilitation Team, the Executive Committee and the Bishops' Commission recognised that this central concept must inform every aspect of the Plenary Council. The six thematic areas, all prefaced, therefore, by the insight that the Church must be centred in Christ, are as follows: the Church as missionary and evangelising; as inclusive, participatory and synodal; as prayerful and Eucharistic; as humble, healing and merciful; as a joyful, hope-filled servant community; and as open to conversion, renewal and reform.

While individuals and communities around Australia continued to reflect on these six thematic areas, writing groups for each of the themes were formed, following an application process open to all members of the Catholic community. Each writing group was made up primarily of lay Catholics and also included one or two bishops. The task of each group was to produce a *Thematic Discernment Paper* that represented a faithful and prayerful discernment of the contributions of the Catholic people of Australia. These papers, together with a Reflection Guide, were published on Pentecost Sunday, 2020. They represent an important 'next step' in the ongoing and hopefully ever-deepening discernment which is at the heart of the Plenary Council journey.

Even though the Church in Australia is engaged in a Plenary Council and not a Synod the decision was made to utilise the synodal practice of preparing an *Instrumentum Laboris,* or *Working Document,* which attempts to bring together in one place the essential insights of the whole journey of discernment thus far and, at the same time, invite the Catholic community into a deeper consideration of the issues, challenges and opportunities before us. This working document entitled *Continuing the Journey* represents, in conjunction with the results of the *Listening and Dialogue* and *Listening and Discernment* processes and the six *Thematic Discernment Papers,* yet a further step in the discernment process leading up to the first assembly.

Prior to the commencement of the first assembly the Steering Committee modified the programme for the assembly in light of the changes required by the new 'on-line' format which had of necessity been adopted. At the same time an agenda sub-committee finalised a proposed agenda for the bishops to consider. Throughout the country local diocesan coordinators, in conjunction with the Facilitation Team, coordinated the provision of formation for the Plenary Council members who lived in their geographical location. This formation was both practical, in terms of training people in the use of the technology required for participation in the assembly, and theological and spiritual. Underpinning all of these endeavours was the commitment to ensure that, notwithstanding the difficulties and challenges of the pandemic and its consequences, the Church in Australia was engaged in one Plenary Council for the whole Church rather than a series of diocesan councils, largely independent of each other.

The decision to postpone the Council for a year thus presented both challenges and opportunities. Most importantly, this decision gave more time to prepare for the first assembly, allowing for a deeper formation in the 'art of discernment' which has been progressively recognised as the heart of our Plenary Council journey.

Because the question guiding us through the experience of the Plenary Council invites us to discern what God is asking of us in Australia at this time, we must remember that 'the Church has always had the duty of scrutinising the signs of the times and of interpreting them in the light of the Gospel' (*Gaudium et Spes,* 4). The extensive consultation process, with its many diverse elements, has sought to respond to this invitation, and the *Working Document* seeks to bring much of this work together. While the signs of the times are numerous, and the national consultation highlighted many of them, one in particular has demanded particular attention: the shocking experience of the sexual abuse of the young, and the inadequate ways in which the Church, especially through some of its leaders, responded to this issue.

In November 2012, Julia Gillard, the Australian Prime Minister at that time, announced the establishment of a Royal Commission into Institutional Responses to Child Sexual Abuse. The dreadful and ongoing suffering of the victims and survivors of sexual abuse, and the often hopelessly inadequate ways in which many Church leaders responded, were laid bare for the whole country to see. A blinding light was shone on the dark places of the Church's life in Australia. The need to respond, through an unflinching acknowledgement of the failures, and to take steps first and foremost to help the survivors of abuse, and then to address the root causes of this disaster, was both obvious and urgent. This was made abundantly clear by the Final Report of the Royal Commission which was presented to the Governor-General of Australia on 15 December 2017 and made public shortly thereafter.

Throughout the six years of the Royal Commission's work the whole Catholic community recognised that this was a 'crisis' moment in the life of the Church in Australia. For this reason, and because the outcome of the Royal Commission would inevitably have serious consequences for the Church, the bishops decided to postpone a final decision on the dates of the Plenary Council until the Royal Commission had concluded. The eventual decision to hold the first assembly in October of 2020 gave us nearly three years in which to begin to understand the implications of the Royal Commission for the life of the Church. Because of this, we were able, in the assembly, to gather the fruits of these years of reflection on this crisis in all its dimensions, including an honest evaluation of our past practices and the suitability of our current and proposed procedures and policies. While what emerged in the first assembly must now be further discerned and developed into concrete proposals for the second assembly to consider, there is an unshakeable consensus among the members of the Plenary Council that the present and the future must be completely different from the past. All members of the council understand that a key part of our responsibility as the Plenary Council process unfolds is the urgent need to continue to scrutinise this devastating sign of the times and interpret it in the light of the Gospel.

Similarly, the experience of the pandemic itself, and the Church's response to it, is clearly a sign of the times to which the Council must attend. We are being called to be open and flexible in regard to new possibilities for mission and evangelisation as we grapple with the 'new normal' as it emerges.

In both of these areas, and in many of the other 'signs of the times' identified in the national consultation and in the *Working Document,* questions relating to both structures and culture within the Church have been acknowledged. These two issues emerged forcefully in the deliberations of the Royal Commission. In response, the bishops commissioned a formal, independent Governance Review. Its final report, *Light from the Southern Cross,* has become another important resource for the members of the Plenary Council, and indeed for the whole

Catholic community, as we seek to interpret everything in the light of the Gospel. Once again, the significance of the Plenary Council's guiding question emerges: 'what do you think *God* is asking of us in Australia *at this time?*'

All of this highlights the importance for the Plenary Council of two themes close to the heart of Pope Francis: discernment and synodality. The two concepts, which are intimately related to each other, offer both possibilities and challenges for the Church in Australia as the Plenary Council experience unfolds. They were certainly very much on the agenda during the first assembly. They will continue to guide and challenge us, not only during the second and final assembly in July 2022, but also in the intervening eight months of ongoing reflection and discussion, and in the implementation of the Plenary Council in the years ahead.

In relation to synodality, Pope Francis has made it clear that careful and comprehensive listening is an essential dimension of this way of being the Church. In the preparations for the Council we have tried to capture something of this in two phrases: *listening to God by listening to each other* and *every voice matters*. Pope Francis explains synodality in this way:

> A synodal Church is a Church which listens, which realises that listening 'is more than simply hearing'. It is a mutual listening in which everyone has something to learn. The faithful people, the college of bishops, the Bishop of Rome: all listening to each other, and all listening to the Holy Spirit, the "Spirit of Truth" (Jn 14:17), in order to know what he 'says to the Churches' (Rev 2:7).[163]

The experience of the national consultation has helped us understand just how complex this process is. A careful analysis of the submissions reveals the wide diversity of views, many of them mutually contradictory, which continues to surface as the members of the

---

163 Pope Francis, 'Address Commemorating the Fiftieth Anniversary of the Institution of the Synod of Bishops', Paul VI Audience Hall, Vatican City, 17 October 2015.

Catholic community 'listen to each other'. Equally, such an analysis invites the question of how successful or otherwise we have been in listening to all the voices. Australia is a multi-cultural nation and the Catholic Church in Australia is a multi-cultural Church. Early in the devising of the consultation process, we were alerted to the possibility that we might end up hearing only, or primarily, the 'white, educated, affluent voice of the Church'. In spite of our best efforts to avoid this, and notwithstanding the high level of response to the national consultation, we must acknowledge that we have not, in fact, heard all the voices because for a variety of reasons, which themselves may constitute a 'sign of the times', so many Catholics were unable to be engaged or chose not to respond. This was recognised during the first assembly: it will be interesting to see how this reality is addressed as we move forward.

This is where the concept of synodality and the concept of discernment interact. As someone intimately involved in the work of the Plenary Council, I often find myself asking how we are to 'catch' the voice of the Holy Spirit speaking in and through the multiplicity of voices to which we are trying to listen. It cannot simply be a matter, as Pope Francis has indicated, of determining the majority opinion and committing to that. Speaking to the bishops of the Synod of the Ukrainian Greek-Catholic Church he stressed the following:

> There is a danger: to think, today, that making a synodal journey or having an attitude of synodality means to sound peoples' opinions, what this or that person thinks, and then to hold a meeting, to agree … No, the Synod is not a Parliament! Things must be said, discussed as normal but it is not a Parliament. The Synod is not about reaching agreement as in politics: I give you this, in exchange for that. No. The Synod is not about making a sociological survey as some would suppose: "Let's see, we'll ask a group of lay people to make an inquiry, to find out if we should change this, this and this." You certainly need to know what your lay people are thinking, but it is not an inquiry; it

is different. If there is no Holy Spirit, there is no Synod. If the Holy Spirit is not present, there is no synodality.[164]

We must continue to ask ourselves, therefore, what else we must bring to the challenge of the Plenary Council to ensure that our discernment enables us to 'test the spirits to see whether they are from God' (1 Jn 4:1).

The first formal assembly of the Plenary Council concluded with a 'live-streamed' Mass from Saint Stephen's Cathedral in Brisbane, celebrated by Archbishop Mark Coleridge, the president of the Australian Catholic Bishops Conference. The assembly was certainly not without its challenges. Some were of a technical and practical nature caused largely by the constraints imposed on us by the Covid-19 pandemic. Others were of a more profound nature. In my own estimation they arose from our struggle to appreciate fully and implement faithfully the call to be a 'synodal Church' as Pope Francis understand this. Deep and open-hearted listening to each other within the mystery of the Lord's Church, in order to hear the voice of the Holy Spirit, is the challenge which lies ahead of us. As the Church in Australia continues along its synodal journey of discernment as to what God is calling us to at this time in our history we are challenged to remain open to the guiding force of the Holy Spirit. The Spirit speaks to us through Jesus as the revelation of the Father; the Spirit is alive in the Church now as in the past; the Spirit is prompting us to scrutinise the signs of the times in the light of the Gospel. Through our openness to the Spirit of God in all the ways in which the Spirit speaks to us we can, together, discover what God is asking of us in Australia at this time.

(Full details concerning the Plenary Council in Australia can be accessed at: www.plenarycouncil.catholic.org.au)

---

164 Pope Francis, 'Address to Bishops of the Synod of the Ukrainian Greek-Catholic Church', Consistory Hall, Vatican City, 2 September 2019.

Questions

- *The Australian Church has identified six themes for reflection. What themes might the Irish church include in its discernment process?*

- *A key phrase emerging from the Australian process is 'every voice matters'. How might a synodal process ensure that voices from all sectors of society are heard?*

11

THE DIOCESAN SYNOD: SYNODALITY IN THE LOCAL CHURCH

Éamonn Fitzgibbon

Éamonn Fitzgibbon is a priest of the Limerick diocese and was director of the Limerick diocesan Synod from 2014 to 2016. In this chapter he outlines the essential practical ingredients that make for a successful diocesan synod – the building blocks which form the process leading to the event itself. He also considers what is involved in a truly synodal way of working together as Church. Finally, he outlines the differences between a formal Diocesan Synod from other Diocesan 'Synodal' Assemblies.

Fr Fitzgibbon holds a doctorate in pastoral theology from the Milltown Institute (UCD). He is a Vicar General of the Limerick diocese as well as a fulltime member of the Department of Theology and Religious Studies at Mary Immaculate College, University of Limerick, where he directs the Irish Institute for Pastoral Studies. He is also a member of the Irish Episcopal Conference's Task Force for the implementation of the Synodal Pathway.

In what follows I wish to say something of what is involved in a diocesan synod, drawing on my experience as director of the Limerick Diocesan Synod in 2016. However, in outlining the steps towards a diocesan synod and the synod event itself, I want to emphasise that in a sense a synod is to synodality what a sacrament is to sacramentality; a synod gives expression to synodality, to what should be a way of being, a continuous style or *modus operandi* in the Church. At the outset, it is important to note that a synod is not just an event – it is also a process; an experience of walking together as a community. This is congruent with the image of Church put before us in Vatican II – the Church as a pilgrim people, as exiles journeying in a foreign land (LG 6), believing that we are led by the Spirit, deciphering signs of God's presence and purpose in the happenings, needs, and desires of this people (GS II).

Guidance

If a synod is a journey then there are a number of maps and guide-books to keep one on track with the design and delivery of a diocesan synod. We find that nine canons are dedicated to the Diocesan Synod in the Code of Canon Law. These canons are worthy of careful study: for example, Canon 460 uses the term *coetus* or assembly to describe the essential characteristic, not the meeting per se, so clearly people are placed above structure. Canon 462 describes the synod as a representative gathering. These canons are explicated in the Instruction on Diocesan Synods, published by the Congregation for Bishops in 1997. Furthermore, Article 163 of The Pastoral Ministry of Bishops (1974) reminds us that the synod is an assembly by which the Bishop fulfils his ministry in adapting the law to local conditions and articulating a programme of pastoral work. It adds that a synod can give impetus to diocesan projects and policies.

Purpose

Essentially a diocesan synod provides the local faith community with an opportunity for renewal, reform and development, establishing a unified diocesan vision addressing the challenges of a particular context. Following the event of a diocesan synod, the diocese should then have a set of diocesan statutes applying the universal law to the local reality and a pastoral plan outlining the intended response to pastoral needs and priorities. Thus, there is a blending of the pastoral, visionary elements with the legislative and the procedural. It provides an opportunity to promote participation, dialogue, listening, discernment and renewal. The Instruction on Diocesan Synods speaks of a diocesan synod shaping pastoral activities, proposing new pastoral plans and expanding and reworking norms as necessary:

> The synod assembly will consider the universal law (or central authority, if you will) and particularize it for the local Church, looking to the needs of God's people in the present and as they walk to the future. The preparation, the process, and the synod assembly will be opportunities to express and celebrate the identity and nature of the local Church and the gifts of the members who create that faith community. As the Code of Canon Law envisions the diocesan synod, it is a body that is representative and a process that is consultative.[165]

Membership

In terms of membership of the synod, the 1983 Code broadened the representation to include laity. Indeed, Canon 463 mandates that certain lay members of the Christian faithful must be invited and the bishop may also invite non-Catholic observers. *The Instruction on Diocesan Synods* offers guidance on selecting lay members by recommending the same criteria outlined in Canon 512 for membership of Diocesan Pastoral Councils be applied. The expectation is that synod membership would reflect the whole face of the diocese and give further support to the notion of a synod as a vehicle for broad-based participation. Over the years the make-up of diocesan synods has greatly changed and nowadays the number of laity present generally far outweighs the clerics present.

---

165 Rehrauer Ann E., 'The Diocesan Synod', *CLSA Proceedings of the Forty-Ninth Annual Convention, 1987*
(Canon Law Society of America, Washington, DC.), 2.

Furthermore, the Instruction speaks of the need to nominate other members paying particular attention to aspects of life not sufficiently represented among the membership through parishes, thus giving adequate expression to the true make-up of the diocese. Thus, synod members fall into a number of categories: there are members who are there by virtue of the office they hold, those who are elected by various groups or individuals, those who are designated by the diocesan bishop, and finally those who can be invited to attend as observers.

In Limerick we wished to ensure that the life of the diocese was truly reflected in our synod membership. Delegates were drawn from parishes, schools (primary and secondary), Third Level Colleges, Health Care communities, members of the Travelling Community and other minority and migrant communities, youth ministry groups and ecclesial communities such as Muintearas Íosa, Charismatic Renewal and others, the Irish, Polish and other language speaking communities, representatives of the city of Limerick, regeneration areas, the worlds of business, the arts, sports and other areas of culture. In all, the Limerick Diocesan Synod had almost four hundred delegates. As Barbara Cusack has stated,

> If the make-up of the synod is not truly reflective of the face of the diocese, the synod's outcome will likely have less support from the community at large. ... In this regard, we cannot emphasise enough the role of the Preparatory Commission in seeing that the right people are 'at the table'.[166]

We also invited members of other faiths to be present as observers. 'As observers they lack the right to participate in consultative votes,' as Cusack notes, 'but they could be given a right to have a voice in the discussions ... There does not seem to be a provision for the selection of non-Christians as synod observers. However, such a selection would appear to be within the discretion of the diocesan bishop.'[167] The presence of members of Churches or ecclesial communities not in full

166 Cusack Barbara A., 'The Diocesan Synod: A Teachable Moment in the Life of the Local Church', in *The Jurist* 63 (2003), 83.
167 Ibid., 79.

communion with the Catholic Church at the synod was a recognition that they can play an important role in the renewal of the Catholic Church. Prior to the synod event we held a structured conversation with representatives from these faiths. This structured conversation included representatives from Church of Ireland, Presbyterian Church, Methodist Church, Baptist Church and Pentecostal Church. Also, although the law does not include inviting members of non-Christian faiths (as we have seen above), it does not exclude it either, so members of Jewish, Muslim, Bahai, Sheik and Islam faiths were also invited to be part of this structured conversation. From this initial gathering observers to each day of the Synod were nominated and formally invited. They contributed to the discussions and contributions.

The Preparatory Commission

As soon as a bishop convokes a synod he is obliged to establish a preparatory commission. Its role is to assist in organising and preparing the synod. The Instruction says the commission is to reflect the charisms and ministries of the diocese and include expertise on canon law and liturgy. In Limerick the commission had twenty-four members and within this there were a number of sub-commissions. These sub-commissions were free to co-opt others to provide specialist support. The sub-commissions included the Spiritual and Catechetical Sub-Commission, the Liturgy Sub-Commission, the Legal Sub-Commission (canonical and civil), the Youth Sub-Commission, the Statistical Analysis and Data Processing Sub-Commission. The Preparatory Commission, through the various sub-commissions, drew on the skills and resources available throughout the diocese – particularly Mary Immaculate College which provided practical meeting space, theological expertise and best practice in research methodology.

The Preparatory Commission was an essential wing to the process and it collaborated closely with the administrative wing which co-ordinated secretarial responsibilities, recording, communication, event management. The Preparatory Commission met at least once a month and this body was itself in the process of journeying together, growing into its role, creating the way as it progressed towards the Synod event.

Listening and Discerning

The time between the convocation and the synod event is a period of time to be carefully managed. On the one hand, it must not be so rushed that there is no time for real listening and discernment and, on the other hand, there needs to be a momentum generated that carries the process along. The journey towards the Synod provides an opportunity for genuine participation and consultation. This time is an opportunity to truly listen and then discern, thus determining the agenda for the synod event. In Limerick the delegates to the Synod were enabled to listen to the needs and concerns of the community they represented. The data created by such listening generated the raw material, which in turn was coded into themes. Once these issues and themes had been identified, there was an opportunity for catechesis and formation on these topics, ensuring that the discussion on the proposals which ultimately made their way on to the floor of the Synod was an informed one:

> The training of synod delegates who are representatives is critical for the process. Unlike political candidates who run for a particular office and who woo the voters with promises and platforms, synod delegates are called to represent the local church. They may be drawn from a geographic area or a parish or a body, but they are called to represent the good of the local church. In discussion they are called to listen and to speak for the good of the church of Northeast Wisconsin or Western Montana, or the church of Harrisburg – rather than for the good of the presbyteral or pastoral council of a diocese. They need to believe that only when we provide for the good of the local church will the good of a particular group also be accomplished.[168]

To begin with, there needs to be a genuine listening to the widest range of people possible. The *Instruction* encourages broad based

---

168 Rehrauer Ann E., 'The Diocesan Synod', *CLSA Proceedings of the Forty-Ninth Annual Convention, 1987*, (Canon Law Society of America, Washington, DC.), 12.

consultation in an atmosphere of prayerful reflection. [169] The time of listening and discernment needs to be genuine and sincere. It must not be controlled or manipulated.

> There is little good to be served if the synod is proposed as participatory in nature but through the preparatory process and the synod sessions dialogue is not encouraged or the atmosphere of a trust-filled exchange is not present. If lip-service is given to the consultation process but the experience is that decisions have already been made and action steps decided upon, it will be challenging to enlist the participation of the faithful. The diocese could lose an important opportunity for ongoing renewal.[170]

We offered a variety of listening methods – eight in all – to the delegates and they in turn engaged with some five thousand people. A working group was established to study and summarise the results of the listening exercises – a not insignificant task, given the huge volume of material gathered. The data fell broadly under twelve thematic headings. The success of this particular undertaking was evidenced in a gathering of delegates in October 2015 wherein there was a strong sense that the listening had been honoured and the voice of the people of Limerick gathered in a clear manner. At this meeting delegates were now tasked with discernment and decision on what topics would be addressed at the Synod. Delegates were asked to prioritise six themes as it was felt this was the most that could reasonably be managed over a three-day Synod. A simple method of discernment was offered to the delegates – a method that was prayerful and reflective and offered a practical experience of discernment-in-action. There followed a period of catechesis for delegates during which they probed their own understanding of the issues that had emerged. This enabled them to get beyond the surface and probed needs and concerns facing the diocese at a deeper level. A variety of teaching moments were offered to delegates in which speakers with expertise gave various inputs on

---

169 Cusack Barbara A., 'The Diocesan Synod: A Teachable Moment in the Life of the Local Church', 80.
170 Ibid., 82-83.

the theological background and the reality of the Limerick context in relation to the themes.

A key feature of a synodal process is prayerful discernment, reminding us that all of this is to be guided by the Spirit – it is God's work and not the result of our efforts alone. Alongside the various inputs, the listening and the learning there is need of space for the Holy Spirit to lead and to respond. This involves a willingness to become aware of one's own biases, attachments and agendas and allow the deeper desires of our heart to be heard.

Once the final six themes were selected, delegates were invited into a process leading to the development of concrete proposals. Once these were submitted (and duplicates and overlaps were edited), a Synod Workbook was produced detailing some one hundred specific proposals, which were in turn voted on at the synod itself. The workbook was distributed to all delegates one week before the synod event and it also contained further background information on the themes and detailed a process for praying, discerning and voting.

Event

At the end of this synodal journey the Diocesan Synod takes place. This usually happens in the format of a large gathering of delegates over a number of days. *The Synod Directory* is helpful in determining the procedure to be followed in the Synod event.

> The preparatory commission should carefully plan the manner in which the synod sessions will proceed and clearly establish the procedural norms. The matters to be studied at the synod arise from and are shaped by the experience of the local church. In order that the fullest experience of the synodal process might be possible, Canon 465 assures that the members of the synod have the right to discuss freely the matters before the synod. Such free discussion would preclude the devolution of the

synod into merely a perfunctory gathering designed to rubber stamp decisions already made.[171]

The Limerick Diocesan Synod met for three days in April 2016. We needed to think carefully about the venue for the synod as we required a space that would facilitate the process of discussion and voting to be used.

> The site for the celebration of the synod also needs to take into consideration the size of the synod and the discussion format in order to facilitate and not inhibit participation. The 1997 Instruction notes that the cathedral should be the site for at least some of the synod sessions as it is the place of the *cathedra* and the visible image of the bishop's authority.[172]

The Synod opened and closed in St John's Cathedral, Limerick with a liturgical celebration but the three-day event took place in Mary Immaculate College where there was ample space, resources and technological support to enable the event to run smoothly. In trying to strategically plan for the future of the diocese from the work of the synod, those present needed to truly strive for consensus.

The diocesan synod will gather members from various parishes and areas of the diocese. The needs of many may be similar, but there will be differences and members will come with a special parochial sensitivity. These must give way to the common good if the synod body is to fashion a vision and pastoral plan reflective of the diversity and the unity of the local Church. There is the commitment of synod members to create pastoral priorities and legislative documents by which they will govern their life as a local Church.[173]

Voting on each of the proposals took place over the first two days. To work through one hundred proposals in a prayerful, calm and participative manner was a challenge. The voting itself was conducted by means of electronic voting devices, which provided immediate

171 Ibid, 81.
172 Ibid., 83, 84.
173 Rehrauer Ann E., "The Diocesan Synod", 2.

responses to each proposal and ensured that everyone was engaged and interested throughout as the results of each vote appeared on the screen. Prior to casting votes, delegates received a brief presentation on the vision underpinning each set of proposals and their connection to the data generated by the listening. There was time for personal reflection, group discussion and open forum. Canon 465 reminds us: 'All questions proposed are to be subject to the free discussion of the members in the session of the synod.' The open forum was a very respectful space where differing and opposing views were expressed in an environment which encouraged deep listening and careful discernment.

The third and final day of the gathering was an opportunity to attend to those issues which juridically cannot be voted on at the synod event. We were conscious of the directive in the Instruction:

> In view of the bonds uniting the particular Church and her Pastor with the universal Church and the Roman Pontiff, the Bishop has the duty to exclude from the synodal discussions theses or positions - as well as proposals submitted to the Synod with the mere intention of transmitting to the Holy See "polls" in their regard – discordant with the perennial doctrine of the Church, the Magisterium or concerning material reserved to Supreme ecclesiastical authority or to other ecclesiastical authorities.

At the same time, we wanted to honour the listening process that had generated responses (and strong feelings) on matters related to the Universal Church and beyond the scope of a Diocesan Synod. This includes the following: clerical celibacy, married priests, women priests, the appointment of bishops, communion for those in second relationships, divorce and remarriage in church, and the new translation of the Mass. The decision was taken that time would be given to discuss such issues in an open and truthful manner.

There weren't any proposals as such on these matters and there was no voting. However, there was an opportunity to share and listen to the views and experiences of delegates on these generative issues. The Bishop committed to including as part of his final report a summary of this conversation. It was a testament to the journey the delegates had been on that this third day was conducted in an atmosphere of respectful and honest sharing and listening. Immediately following the event, the Synod documents were prepared and finalised. These include a set of Diocesan Statutes and the Diocesan Pastoral Plan. Along with the documentation forwarded to the Papal Nuncio was the summary from Bishop Brendan outlining the discussion on the Universal Issues of Day Three as outlined above. The Diocesan Pastoral Plan continues to guide the work of the diocese and Rose O'Connor has been employed to oversee its implementation. Indeed, the delivery of this plan was evaluated twelve months after its launch and continues to be reviewed on a regular basis.

Conclusion

The question is often asked: 'What is the difference between a diocesan assembly and a diocesan synod?' In my experience, it is important to recognise and value the many diocesan assemblies that have taken place in Ireland over the last twenty years or so. They are truly synodal moments. It is not my intention to suggest that one approach is more worthy than another, rather, it is for each diocese to discern the approach most appropriate to its own particular circumstances. In Limerick we had already conducted a diocesan Listening Process back in 1997 and subsequently conducted a deep listening process among clergy and diocesan staff in 2008. It seemed to us that a synod was the next logical step. As I mentioned at the outset a synod is intended to produce a pastoral plan and a set of statutes – it generates a new pastoral approach and the local norms to implement this. We read in the prologue to the *Instruction*: 'In recent times it is noted that expressions of diocesan communion have also adopted other forms, sometimes described as "diocesan assemblies". While such assemblies often include elements of diocesan Synods, they do, however, lack a precise canonical character.' In my experience, a synod carries a more weight, has greater authority and thus stands a better chance of engendering real change. However, it is only in the years ahead that we will be truly able to assess the impact of the Limerick Diocesan Synod 2016.

Questions

- *According to Article 163 of The Pastoral Ministry of Bishops (1974), the synod is an assembly by which the Bishop fulfils his ministry in adapting the law to local conditions and articulating a programme of pastoral work. What local conditions might be specific to your diocese as you journey together towards a more synodal church?*

- *Members of other churches were invited to be part of the listening and discussion processes leading up to the Limerick diocesan synod. Thinking of other faiths in your local community, how might they enhance the synodal process in Ireland?*

12

SYNODALITY: HOW MANAGEMENT AND LEADERSHIP THEORY CAN CONTRIBUTE TO DISCERNING THE *SIGNS OF THE TIMES*.

Janet Forbes

Janet Forbes is a graduate student at Boston College's School of Theology and Ministry with research interests in Synodality, Ecclesiology, Catechetics, Communication, and Inculturation. In this chapter she explores the commonalities between reform in the Church and in the world of business in terms of leadership and organisational development. She focuses on how leaders can communicate effectively, inspire vision and involve people appropriately in decision-making processes.

The author is a graduate of the University of Ulster who previously worked in the BMW network and who also holds a qualification in pastoral theology from St Patrick's College, Maynooth.

On the fiftieth anniversary of the institution of the Synod of Bishops, Pope Francis stated, 'It is precisely this path of synodality which God expects of the Church of the third millennium.'[174] Francis's pontificate, framed within the current change of era heralded by the Second Vatican Council, is characterised by a mandate of reform coupled with a reimagining of what it means to be Church amidst a 'new phase of reception' of the Council.[175] It is clear that the theology underpinning the council has solidified as an understanding that, with the Council, we experienced a movement towards the reality of a global Church.[176] The question now critically turns to how we create such a vision of Church. Rafael Luciani articulates the view that this chapter involves meaningful integration of the vision and spirit of the Second Vatican Council in concrete and real terms. The Venezuelan theologian states that this reimagining of structures and processes, coupled to much-needed reframing of mindsets, is marked by a space of openness and creative innovation regarding existing processes and practices within the Church.[177] In this essay, I utilise the co-partnered disciplines of Leadership and Management in an endeavour to address the question of how we can realise the vision articulated throughout the Second Vatican Council and its reception. I also discuss how such disciplines offer wisdom for reading the context and markers of the world we live in and practical tools for synodal practice.

Joseph De Smedt, Bishop of Bruges, appealed to the Council on December 1st 1962 that the Second Vatican Council should 'terminate the triumphalist, clerical and juridical appearance of the Church'.[178]

174 Pope Francis, *Ceremony Commemorating The 50th Anniversary of The Institution of The Synod of Bishops* (17 October 2015), 2015. *Vatican. Va.* http://www.vatican.va/content/francesco/en/speeches/2015/october/documents/papa-francesco_20151017_50-anniversario-sinodo.html.

175 Rafael Luciani, 'Is Querida Amazonia the Beginning of a Creative New Reception of the Synodal Path?' (Part 1)' *Doctrine and Life*, 71, (2020), 1-2.

176 Karl Rahner, 'Towards a Fundamental Theological Interpretation of the Vatican II', *Theological Studies* 40 (1979), 716-727.

177 Rafael Luciani, 'Is Querida Amazonia the Beginning of a Creative New Reception of the Synodal Path?' (Part 1)', 1-4.

178 Myriam Wijlens, 'Reform and renewal implementing Vatican II', in Carlos M. Galli and Antonio Spadaro SJ, *For a Missionary reform of the Church*. The Civiltà Cattolica Seminar, Paulist Press, NY 2017, 336-357.

It strikes me that this appeal and the Council itself were prophetic, for neither Bishop De Smedt nor the Council fathers could foresee the change and challenge that lay ahead. It is clear when reflecting on the intervening years that the need for reform within the Church has become an imperative. In the years since the Council, this movement to reform rigid and inflexible structures and processes has also been experienced and enacted within other areas of life and business. This parallel activity points to the fact that Bishop De Smedt's appeal addresses hierarchical and clericalist mentalities, and signposts more general issues that reflect the world the Council fathers faced and indeed the context of the world today. Contextually within the Church, such concerns relate directly to the transmission of the Gospel in real terms, therefore necessitating urgent attention.

In *Evangelii Gaudium*, Pope Francis addresses the crisis of communal commitment, acknowledging that 'humanity is experiencing a turning-point in its history' and that 'the joy of living frequently fades' amidst an era of epochal change that has 'set in motion enormous qualitative, quantitative, rapid and cumulative advances in the sciences and in technology'.[179] In truth, we find ourselves unable to cognitively frame our role in the world as Christian community,[180] and it is clear, from Pope Francis's perspective, that the institutional model of Church is failing and simply not able to cope with the demands placed on it by our current reality. Simply put, the Church is no longer able to adequately transmit the Christian message in the third millennium. I suggest that we are better able to understand the unwillingness to engage with the Church within the framework of a crisis of transmission of faith and not simply a crisis of faith.

In *Evangelii Gaudium*, Francis challenges, among other things, individualism, the lack of respect for the human person, financial and economical frameworks that dominate, and the growth of consumerism

---

179 Pope Francis, *Evangelii Gaudium : Apostolic Exhortation on The Proclamation of The Gospel in Today's World. Vatican. Va.* 2013, 52, http://www.vatican.va/content/francesco/en/apost_exhortations/documents/papa-francesco_esortazione-ap_20131124_evangelii-gaudium.html.

180 See, Kegan, Robert *In Over Our Heads*, (Cambridge, Massachusetts, Harvard University Press, 1994).

and populism in the world. One argument I offer within the context of this essay is that, contrary to popular perceptions, such difficulties have also been reflected on and challenged within secular disciplines. I note that many organisations and individuals hold views consistent with those of Pope Francis and have even moved into a space whereby concrete plans and action are being formulated to tackle such challenges. In the period since the end of the Council a quiet revolution has been occurring in progressive circles associated with the disciplines of Economics, Leadership, and Management, one that is marked by an admission that old paradigms and mindsets created during the enlightenment are also no longer fit for purpose. Some notable protagonists within this group are economists Kate Raworth and Joseph Stiglitz who respectively acknowledge in their works, Doughnut Economics[181] and People, Power and Profits,[182] the failures of aggressive economic models, and strongly challenge the disparities that exist in our world. Each highlights abuses of power, offering alternative models designed to integrate justice, equity and the development of robust ethical frameworks. When considered in a complimentary fashion with the teaching of Pope Francis, they offer concrete solutions to those problems we seek to challenge in the Church, along with affirmation of our current reading of the Signs of the Times.

Of significance for this conversation is the fact that, within these disciplines, processes and practices designed to assist thorough analysis of the context are at an advanced stage, providing reasons for the breakdown of old models, with many leaders exhibiting profound willingness to adapt structures and practices in ways necessitated by changing circumstances. Within the best examples offered in the field of Leadership and Management rigorous analysis of the cultural context is the norm and has resulted in perpetual rationalisation and differentiation of processes, structures and practices, so that anything non-essential to the primary mission and stated values is subjected to change. This openness and ability to change, with its orientation towards the overarching mission of the organisation and the flourishing of people therein, draws

---

181 New York: Random House Business, 2017.
182 New York: W. W. Norton and Company, 2019.

direct parallels with the ministry of Pope Francis. This in itself offers insight for those in positions of leadership within the Church affirming the mechanisms of synodality that now take root.

Eduardo P. Braun, a former director of HSM group, leadership expert and author of People First Leadership, lays out five roles of leadership that mark the shift experienced in the fields of Leadership and Management. These are the ability to: 'inspire a vision', 'being all about your people', and understanding the role of 'communication' in elaborating a vision and in relations with people. Braun also gives critical consideration to understanding the importance of 'decision making', issues of official and unofficial power relating to it, and the development of culturally appropriate frameworks for decision making that sufficiently encompass 'culture' and 'people', both in terms of reading and managing both.[183] In People First Leadership it is telling that Braun utilises Pope Francis as a paradigm of 'new leadership exemplified'[184] stating that 'in the end leadership comes down to being an agent of change, whether it's shifting vision or radically altering hundreds of years of social and cultural practice'.[185] For too long in the Church we have perhaps focused on management of resources in the fiscal realm to the detriment of articulating our ultimate vision and navigating towards that North Star.

I am aware that many will challenge my endeavours to draw parallels between the disciplines of Leadership and Management and the task of reforming the Church through pastoral conversion and synodal practice.[186] Central to any meaningful integration of this work is the understanding that the source of the vision and mission of the Church is what ultimately differentiates our endeavours from those operating within the realms of Leadership and Management. Crucial to my argument is a fundamental understanding that all we do in Church finds its source in God, with all agency imbued by God through the

---

183 Eduardo P. Braun. *People First Leadership : How the Best Leaders Use Culture and Emotion to Drive Unprecedented Results.* (New York: McGraw-Hill Education), 2017.
184 Ibid., 266.
185 Ibid., 266.
186 Piero Coda. 'The Way of the Church in the third Millennium', *Proche-Orient chrétien* 68 (2018), 316- 325.

Holy Spirit. *Lumen Gentium* articulates the Church's mission succinctly when it says that 'proclaiming the Gospel to every creature,
to bring the light of Christ to all' is the Church's North Star.[187] The
question that emerges from such an articulation is how and in what
way we are called to do this in our time. I think that at the root of the
crisis we currently experience lies the fact that we have lost sight of this
primary vision and mission.

Within Leadership and Management, a clear understanding has
emerged that the articulation of an inspirational and aspirational
vision is critical for the empowerment and motivation of human
beings. In these disciplines, it has been found again and again that
participation of all in the elaboration of decisions pertaining to all
directly impacts outcomes and the ultimate realisation of an expressed vision. Those in positions of leadership have direct responsibility for evoking 'emotion' and generating a 'sense of purpose' in
a way that bequeaths agency to all their people. This brings to the
fore the critical issue of how and in what way within Church the
episcopate and those commissioned for leadership understand their
identity and role. It also raises questions around their perceptions
of the role of laity in decision-making and taking. Peter de Mey in
'Sharing the Threefold Office of Christ' highlights a pastoral letter
from Bishop Joseph De Smedt to the Secretariat for Christian Unity
on the main distinction between the royal priesthood of all faithful
and the ordained ministers. De Mey notes that the pastoral letter of
De Smedt reminds its readers that there is but 'One priest: Christ
Jesus', and from this the priestly work of all the faithful emerges.[188]
I believe that the mission and vision are mandated by God and the
work of developing mechanisms for achieving that vision are the
task of all within the Church.

---

187 Pope Paul VI. *Lumen Gentium.* Vatican.Va. 1964. 1 http://www.
vatican.va/archive/hist_councils/ii_vatican_council/documents/
vat-ii_const_19641121_lumen-gentium_en.html.

188 Peter De Mey. 'Sharing in the threefold office of Christ. A different matter for laity
and priests? The tria munera in Lumen gentium, Presbyterorum Ordinis, Apostolicam
Actuositatem and Ad Gentes', in Anne Marie C. Mayer, *The Letter and the Spirit on
the forgotten Documents of Vatican II,* (), 155-179.

Within the wider framework of society and regardless of the discipline, it is undeniable that it is no longer acceptable for decisions
to be taken in isolation by one person or by a few through specific
commission or ordering. The challenge for the Church is to reimagine appropriate frameworks and structures for decision making. St.
Cyprian, who was bishop of Carthage from 248 to 258, left behind
a collection of letters which offer much when considering synodality
and the development of synodal processes, practices and structures
today. St. Cyprian's letters present important insight into the role of
laity in decision-making in the early Church. Saint Cyprian speaks
of the participation of the laity in decision-making in four different
contexts: in the election of a bishop, in appointments to the clergy, in
conciliar decisions, and in the reconciliation of repentant sinners.[189]
Essentially, in the letters of St. Cyprian, we learn that anything that
affected the entirety of the Church in Carthage was 'judged and voted upon by all'.[190] Again, we are not told in the letters the mechanisms through which this judgement was enacted, but we do know
that it mirrored similar practices in Rome. Such historical precedence
and lack of detail affords opportunity to consider other disciplines
and their models of decision-making dialectically. In Leadership and
Management, complex mechanisms and processes of consultation
have taken form and I suggest that adequate consideration of these
methods can help the participation in, elaboration of and taking of
decisions by all people within the Church.

So far I have offered thoughts on the critical role and agency
that all people are given within the disciplines of Leadership and
Management, and I have also presented historical precedents in the
early Church, but I now wish to draw specific focus on the schema
that underpins the Second Vatican Council with regard to people and
their agency within the Church. With the Second Vatican Council, a
shift in how all subjects in the Church were to be viewed occurred.
In *Lumen Gentium*, in which Bishop De Smedt is credited as being
an architect, the structure and ordering of the chapters is deliberate.

189 Ibid.
190 Ibid.

These were debated at length in the council and are crucial to our current understanding of what synodality is and is not. Following an articulation of the nature and mystery of the Church in chapter one of *Lumen Gentium*, chapter two articulates a vision of Church as People of God, whereby all 'holy people of God share in Christ's prophetic office spreading abroad a living witness to Him'[191] and that:

> the entire body of the faithful, anointed as they are by the Holy One, cannot err in matters of belief ... manifesting this special property by means of the whole peoples' supernatural discernment in matters of faith when "from the Bishops down to the last of the lay faithful" show universal agreement in matters of faith and morals.[192]

This understanding of *People of God* is considered the normative key through which we understand the Council and represents a significant shift, because it firstly acknowledges the ability of all to discern the movement of the Spirit and secondly, expresses a horizontal and equitable understanding of the agency all persons hold within the Church. It is this understanding that lies at the core of synodality, specifically the ability of all to discern the movement of the Spirit that mandates change, opening conversations around the mechanisms of how all people are to be included in the discernment of the Spirit, the elaboration of decisions within Church and the future placement of juridical power in the Church.

Within the fields of Leadership and Management a similar movement towards equity and inclusion of all subjects has occurred, but my assessment is that a fully integrated model and schema such as that articulated in the Second Vatican Council has yet to be invoked within the secular realm. However, more progressive organisations realise that if your people are not with you, the organisation experiences great difficulties in realising vision and mission. These organisations

191 Pope Paul VI. *Lumen Gentium*. Vatican.Va. 1964, 12 http://www.vatican.va/archive/hist_councils/ii_vatican_council/documents/vat-ii_const_19641121_lumen-gentium_en.html.
192 Ibid.

have allocated significant resources to the task of respecting people, forming people and helping them thrive in a way that the Church has not. Trust and credibility are taken seriously within exemplar businesses and it is openly stated that without both it is nearly impossible to orientate your people to your mission. The Church could benefit from carefully studying the mechanisms used by organisations within the realm of business and leadership.

This is of critical import because central to the teaching of the Vatican II is an understanding that each person is unique and imbued with specific charisms. Many faithful subjects find their vocation within the field of Leadership and Management utilising these charisms. I question, therefore, if these individuals hold greater expertise, for example, in developing and outlining communication models and designing mechanisms marked by credibility and trust. Austrian educator and management consultant, Peter Drucker, expresses the view that 'people are an organisation's most valuable resource'[193] and Eduardo P. Braun asserts that 'leaders therein champion values'.[194] In light of both statements and in relation to the Church's self-understanding as People of God, is there a treasure trove of skillsets and Charisms waiting to be discovered within the Church, and what mechanisms need to be developed to uncover them? It is a necessary caveat to such assertions that there are distinct divisions within the field of Leadership and Management in specific nations and sectors. Therefore, I suggest that a targeted analysis of processes and mechanisms is required, suggesting that consideration of organisations operating within more equitable market economies such as Germany and Scandinavian block countries would yield wisdom and insight more appropriate to synodality. Such organisations and nations have just and equitable frameworks of governance and leadership. Analysis of such realities can only assist discernment processes and help in clarifying the Church's understanding of the signs of the times. They could also aid the development of practices specifically related to the elaboration and taking of decisions that honour the charisms and agency of all.

---

193 Peter F. Drucker *Management Essentials*. (La Vergne: Harvard Business Review Press, 2020).
194 Eduardo P Braun. *People First Leadership*, 111.

With regard to decision-making and decision-taking within a synodal framework, I believe the current epochal change we are living through represents a significant and notable shift in the reception of the Second Vatican Council, whereby the spirt of episcopal collegiality realised in the institution of the Synod of Bishops by Pope Paul VI has, during Pope Francis's papacy, developed further into what is now understood as collegial synodality. Crucially, with regard to developing a truly synodal Church recent developments in Latin America, specifically with regard to the Synod on the Amazon, mark a move towards what is now termed synodal ecclesiality.[195] Synodal ecclesiality is a reality whereby all persons as equal ecclesial subjects are afforded agency and power with regard to discernment and concrete mechanisms of governance within the Church. It involves discernment by all subjects within the Church about where and how the Spirit moves, and links it to discernment processes designed to enact tangible responses regarding the primary mission of evangelising in a specific and local context. It also marks a shift in real terms to a position whereby every resource, structure, process and practice must be orientated towards this primary mission. It is also marked by its integration of all the People of God in all dimensions of Church life, and not just some by virtue of ordering through ordination.[196] More importantly, ecclesial synodality is significantly marked by a decentralisation whereby local Churches, local bishops and ecclesial bodies are encouraged and empowered to deal with issues specific and unique to their specific cultural context.

Whilst many institutions within the realm of Leadership and Management have not fully adopted such a framework, they have a wealth of experience in decentralised leadership models that are adopted to local contexts and culture, and they are adept at managing their own culture to fit the wider cultural landscape. This may be seen by some as a form of populism, but there is wealth in picking apart

---

195 Rafael Luciani. 'Is Querida Amazonia the Beginning of a Creative New Reception of the Synodal Path? (Part 1)' *Doctrine and Life*. 71, (2020), 1-2.

196 Pope Paul VI. *Lumen Gentium* 12. Vatican.Va. 1964, http://www.vatican.va/archive/hist_councils/ii_vatican_council/documents/vat-ii_const_19641121_lumen-gentium_en.html.

the structures, mechanisms and processes utilised so that wisdom can be gleaned. In this way the processes, practices and mechanisms can be seen as tools that can assist in developing, for example, differentiated listening processes within synodal events. In the same way, such organisations and their utilisation of information technology, specifically processes for *data mining* of publicly available information, could offer access to important information that readily informs the big questions we face in Church. Additionally, within the disciplines of Leaderships and Management, robust frameworks and differentiated models of communication have been developed so that the value of the organisation fits individual cultures and demographics. It is this aspect that could help develop inclusive and safe spaces within which those on the margins and outside the Church could articulate their sense of faith and the reality of their context. Such analysis could also yield practices designed to hold tension between diverse and differing voices within the Church.

Robert Keegan, a developmental psychologist, having looked at our current reality and the multiple hermeneutical frameworks or orders of knowing that exist in it, suggests that if growth and development within humans is to occur in a safe space then sufficient support and challenge need to exist.[197] In a world marked by multiple orders and frameworks for knowing, authenticity and trust are essential and it must be acknowledged that the propensity for conflict amidst difference is increased. Robust frameworks that honour difference and communication models that are cognisant of difference are required if unity in diversity is to be realised within a synodal reality. Throughout this essay, the theme of culture has prevailed with the ability to analyse both current societal and cultural reality in the local Church perceived as a crucial consideration within synodal ecclesiality. Many secular organisations have acknowledged that the world has changed beyond recognition and most have responded to these circumstances by changing their practices, structures and processes so that they better serve their mission. Reading culture is perhaps the single most important area whereby the disciplines of Leadership and Management can help

---

197 Kegan, Robert. *In Over Our Heads*, 342.

develop robust frameworks for assessing the societal landscape, so that the Church may exact necessary and appropriate reforms.

Hermann Pottmeyer, in 'The Church on its Pilgrim Way to Arise as the People of God', states that during the Second Vatican Council 'the desire for reform was not part of the discussion' by the council fathers, but that the question of 'how to assess the contemporary world' was.[198] As I conclude this essay, it is this question that remains foremost, for it lies at the heart of the current debate within the Church, as does the concern for what must change and what is 'binding and unchanging in the Church'.[199] I believe Pottmeyer's insight gives much food for thought when considering the role other disciplines and the many faithful subjects residing therein can play in reforming Church structures as well as developing synodal processes and practices. For many progressive businesses, circular reflection on that which is outdated and no longer fit for purpose has become a way of being. In this reflective reality, a real willingness to constantly let go of those things that no longer serve their values and mission has meant that such organisations have developed robust systems and processes of analysis, designed to articulate the current reality and credible mechanisms for change. When considering the council fathers' concern for that which was bound by 'time and change', as Pottmeyer puts it, I believe wider frameworks of reflection and analysis go beyond traditional mechanisms currently utilised within Church and can assist in breaking new synodal ground. Pedro Arrupe, in a letter to the Society of Jesus in 1978, stated that 'the changes which have taken place, and which will keep on taking place in the future, have their origin in the criteria of Vatican II' and that 'these changes will have no practical effect if we do not allow the transforming power of the Spirit to modify our personal life from within'.[200] In this consideration of the

---

198 Hermann J. Pottmeyer,. 'The Church on its Pilgrim Way to Arise as the People of God' in Antonio Spadaro and Carlos M. Galli, *For a Missionary Reform of the Church*. (The Civiltà Cattolica Seminar, Paulist Press, NJ, 2017), 58.

199 Ibid.

200 Pedro Arrupe. Inculturation to the Whole Society. 'The Portal to Jesuit Studies'. *Jesuitportal.Bc.Edu.*, (1978), https://jesuitportal.bc.edu/research/documents/1978_arrupeinculturationsociety/.

disciplines of Leadership and Management, I have played the devil's advocate in offering creative and perhaps debateable thoughts on how these disciplines offer wisdom within a synodal framework, but I have done so from the perspective of a lay subject with intimate experience of both the disciplines of Leadership and Management and pastoral theology. In conclusion, I acknowledge the critical need for flexibility and openness to other viewpoints that encourage collective change brought about within synodal frameworks.

Questions

- *Many secular organisations have acknowledged that the world has changed beyond recognition and have responded to these circumstances by changing their practices, structures and processes so that they better serve their mission. How might the current synodal process enable a similar response in the Irish Church?*

- *If your people are not with you then your organisation experiences great difficulties in realising its vision and mission. Trust and credibility are paramount. How can the Irish Church rebuild trust and credibility in order to achieve its vision and mission in the future? Will the synodal process enable this?*

⊞ BIBLIOGRAPHY

Arrupe, Pedro. (1978), 'The Portal to Jesuit Studies', in *Jesuitportal.Bc.Edu.* https://jesuitportal.bc.edu/research/documents/1978_arrupeinculturationsociety/.

Braun, Eduardo P. (2017), *People First Leadership: How the Best Leaders Use Culture and Emotion to Drive Unprecedented Results.* New York: McGraw-Hill Education.

Coda, Piero. (2018), 'The Way of the Church in the third Millennium', in *Proche-Orient Chrétien* 68, 316-325.

De Mey, Peter. (2018), 'Sharing in the threefold office of Christ. A different matter for laity and priests? The tria munera in Lumen gentium, Presbyterorum Ordinis, Apostolicam Actuositatem and Ad Gentes', in Anne Marie C. Mayer, *The Letter and the Spirit on the forgotten Documents of Vatican II,* eds. Peeters, Leuven, 155-179.

De Smedt, Emille Joseph. (1962), *The Priesthood of the Faithful,* NY: Paulist Press.

Drucker, Peter F. (2020), *Management Essentials,* La Vergne: Harvard Business Review Press.

Galli, Carlos M. (2017), 'The missionary reform of the Church according to Francis. The Ecclesiology of the Evangelizing People of God', in Antonio Spadaro and Carlos M. Galli eds. *For a Missionary Reform of the Church.* The Civiltà Cattolica Seminar, New Jersey: Paulist Press.

Kegan, Robert. (1994), *In Over Our Heads.* Cambridge, Massachusetts: Harvard University Press.

Hinze, Bradford E. (2006), *Practices of Dialogue in the Roman Catholic Church: Aims and Obstacles, Lessons and Laments.* New York: Continuum.

Hinze, Bradford E. (2020), 'The Grace of Conflict', *Theological Studies* 81, 40-64.

Komonchak, Joseph. (1998), *People of God, Hierarchical Structure, and Communion: An Easy Fit?* in Canon Law Society of America, Proceedings of the Sixteenth Annual Convention, 91-102.

Luciani, Rafael. (2017), *Pope Francis and the Theology of the People.* Maryknoll: Orbis Books.

Luciani, Rafael. (2018), 'The centrality of the People in Pope Francis's Socio-cultural theology', in *Concilium 3,* London: SCM Press, 55-68.

Luciani, Rafael. (2020), 'Is Querida Amazonia the Beginning of a Creative New Reception of the Synodal Path? (Part 1)', in *Doctrine and Life,* Vol 71, Dublin: Dominican Publications Dublin, 1-4.

Mintzberg, Henry. (2015), *Rebalancing Society: Radical Renewal Beyond Left, Right, and Center,* Oakland, CA: Berrett-Koehler Publishers, Inc.

Pottmeyer, Hermann J. (2017), 'The Church on its Pilgrim Way to Arise as the People of God', in Antonio Spadaro and Carlos M. Galli, eds. *For a Missionary Reform of the Church.* The Civiltà Cattolica Seminar, New Jersey: Paulist Press.

Pope Francis. (2013), *Evangelii Gaudium: Apostolic Exhortation on The Proclamation of The Gospel In Today's World. Vatican.* http://www.vatican.va/content/francesco/en/apost_exhortations/documents/papa-francesco_esortazione-ap_20131124_evangelii-gaudium.html.

Pope Francis. 50th Anniversary of the Institution of the Synod of Bishops (On Synodality), 2015.

Pope Paul VI. (1964), *Lumen Gentium.* Vatican.Va. http://www.vatican.va/archive/hist_councils/ii_vatican_council/documents/vat-ii_const_19641121_lumen-gentium_en.html.

Pope Paul VI. (2014), 'International Theological Commission', in *Sensus fidei in the Life of the Church. Vatican. Va.* http://www.vatican.va/roman_curia/congregations/cfaith/cti_documents/rc_cti_20140610_sensus- fidei_en.html.

Pope Paul VI. (2018), 'International Theological Commission', in *Synodality In the Life and Mission of The Church.* Vatican.Va. https://www.vatican.va/roman_curia/congregations/cfaith/cti_documents/rc_cti_20180302_sinodalita_en.html.

Rahner, Karl. (1979), 'Towards a Fundamental Theological Interpretation of the Vatican II', in *Theological Studies* (40), 716-727.

Raworth, Kate. (2017), *Doughnut Economics: Seven Ways to Think Like a 21st Century Economist.* White River Junction, Vermont: Chelsea Green Publishing.

Commonwealth of Australia. (2017), 'Royal Commission into Institutional Responses to Child Sexual Abuse, Final Report', Volume 16, Book 2.

Rush, Ormund. (2001), *Sensus Fidei: faith making sense of Revelation,* Theological Studies 62.

Stiglitz, Joseph E. (2019), *People, Power, and Profits: Progressive Capitalism for an Age of Discontent.* New York: W.W. Norton & Company.

Sullivan, Francis. (2004), 'St. Cyprian on the role of the Laity in Decision Making in the Early Church', in Stephen Pope eds., *Common Calling. The Laity and Governance of the Catholic Church,* Washington: Georgetown University Press, 39-49.

Vitali, Dario. (2017), 'The Circularity Between Sensus Fidei and Magisterium as a Criterion for the Exercise of Synodality in the Church', in Carlos M. Galli and Antonio Spadaro SJ eds., *For a Missionary reform of the Church.* The Civiltà Cattolica Seminar, NY: Paulist Press, 196-217.

Wijlens, Myriam. (2017), 'Reform and renewal implementing Vatican II', in Carlos M. Galli and Antonio Spadaro SJ eds., *For a Missionary reform of the Church.* The Civiltà Cattolica Seminar, NY: Paulist Press, 336-357.

13

AN ENTIRELY SYNODAL CHURCH

Maureen Kelly

Maureen Kelly is Coordinator of Liturgy and Spirituality with the Killaloe Diocese. In this chapter she outlines the particular challenges and crises faced by the Catholic Church in Ireland to which the Synodal Pathway must seek to respond. These include declining practice, aging clergy, loss of credibility and trust, and the legacy of past attempts at reform that failed to deliver what they promised. The author pleads for a listening process that is both honest and authentic and that includes those on the peripheries and a willingness to abandon structures and forms of ministry that can no longer serve the Church's mission.

Maureen Kelly holds MA degrees in Pastoral Ministry from All Hallows College, Dublin and in Leadership and Organisational Development from the Tavistock Institute in London.

The possibilities that the synodal vision of Francis opens up and the profound shift it requires is only gradually coming into view. In effect, he is calling the whole Church, to a new way of being. A few preliminary remarks create the context for reflection on the role of the lay faithful in a synodal Church.

A synodal Church is a Church which listens ... It is a mutual listening in which everyone has something to learn. The faithful people, the college of bishops, the Bishop of Rome: all listening to each other, and all listening to the Holy Spirit, the 'Spirit of truth' (Jn 14:17) in order to know what he "says to the Churches" (Rev 2:7).[201]

It calls for a wholly participant Church, in which all God's people are subjects, 'by virtue of the dignity of their baptism and their friendship with Christ' and 'through their sharing in the one priesthood of Christ'.[202] 'In all the baptized, from first to last, the sanctifying power of the Spirit is at work, impelling us to evangelization. The people of God is holy thanks to this anointing.'[203]

The anointing of the Holy Spirit is manifested in the 'sensus fidei' – an instinct of faith which allows them to discern what is truly of God.[204]

Synodality is in the service of mission. It is not an end in itself, but should lead the Church to reaching out beyond itself in mission. All are called to mission, so all must listen and discern together where the Holy Spirit is leading the Church.

A Synodal Pathway for a Church in Crisis

Against this backdrop, the Irish Bishops have announced their intention to embark on a synodal pathway for the Irish Church and to hold a National Synodal Assembly within the next five years. The context in which the Irish Church is embarking on this path is stark. There is widespread recognition that the Irish Church is in deep crisis

201 Pope Francis, Address commemorating the 50th Anniversary of the Synod of Bishops, October 2015. See https://www.vatican.va/content/francesco/en/speeches/2015/october/documents/papa-francesco_20151017_50-anniversario-sinodo.html.
202 International Theological Commission. 'Synodality in the Life and Mission of the Church' (2018), 17.
203 Evangelii Gaudium, 119.
204 'Synodality in the Life and Mission of the Church', 56.

and there is a longing for leadership and a collective response. The Church system as we have known it is broken. The service model of Church, which came into being as Irish society recovered from the famine, and which thrived for most of the twentieth century, is in free fall. The now Archbishop of Dublin (and then Bishop of Ossory) put it succinctly: 'The Catholic Church in Ireland is in the maelstrom of its gravest crisis in centuries.'[205] If the synodal path is to address this situation, it is crucial that the depth of the crisis be acknowledged.

There is a crisis of participation. Dr Michael Breen's work on patterns of religious practice in Ireland, based on the European Values Studies, allows us to sketch the fall in weekly Mass attendance between 1981 and 2018.[206] Below are the figures for six age cohorts from 18–25-year-olds to those over 65:

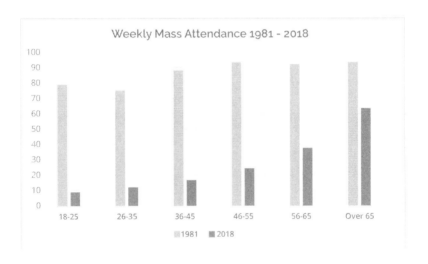

Over four decades, participation in Sunday Eucharist, has dropped dramatically and in some age cohorts has completely collapsed. It is

205 Archbishop Dermot Farrell, address to Conference with Laity and Priests in the Diocese of Ossory. https://ossory.ie/2018/11/conference-of-laity-and-priests-of-the-diocese-of-ossory-exploring-our-parishes-today/.
206 The data quoted here is from a lecture given by Dr Michael Breen on Religious Practice in Ireland 1979 - 2019 as part of the Mary Immaculate College Certificate in Pastoral Ministry, November 2020.

widely anticipated that the decline will be accelerated following from the COVID pandemic.

This profoundly impacts on the local Church. Numbers regularly participating in the life of their local parish communities continue to decline. The pool of people available as volunteers for parish groups and programmes is also declining and aging. Many priests, lay ministers and volunteers continue in parish roles because there is no one to take their place. Allied to the decline in participation is a decline in financial support for the Church.

The crisis is also apparent in relation to priesthood. In the diocese of Killaloe, over one third of parishes are currently without a resident priest. My experience is of a tiredness and discouragement among many priests, many of whom carry on valiantly, trying to shore up a dying system. Discouragement makes it hard to generate energy or hope about the possibility of change.

In his speech marking the visit of Pope Francis to Ireland in 2018, the Taoiseach, Leo Varadkar, publicly recognised the contribution the Church had made to the benefit of many generations, filling gaps in education, healthcare and social services not provided for by the State. Revelations of abuse in religious-run institutions along with clerical child sexual abuse has, however, obliterated the memory of the good work done by priests and religion, and severely damaged the respect in which they and the Church at large were once held. Where the Church occupied a central, respected and dominant position in Irish Society, now, in many instances, it perceives the environment as hostile and unsupportive. In the past few decades, Church in Ireland has gone from having a powerful presence with influence and energy to being a much depleted, older, less energised Church, with an uncertain view of its place in Irish society.

On the other hand, there are still significant numbers of people for whom belief in God, prayer and living of the Gospel in their everyday lives gives meaning and hope. Dr Michael Breen points to an interesting finding of the European Values Study. The graph below compares data on participation in weekly Mass side by side with data on the practice of weekly prayer for 2018, the most recent year of the European Values Study.

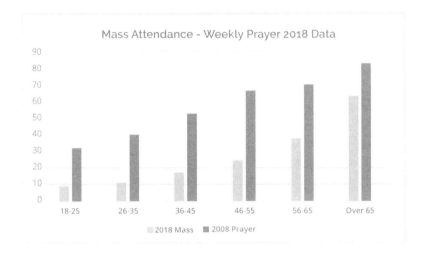

Mass Attendance - Weekly Prayer 2018 Data
(2018 Mass, 2008 Prayer; ages 18-25, 26-35, 36-45, 46-55, 56-65, Over 65)

Figures for non-participation at Mass do not necessarily mean the rejection of God. Even a significant number of younger people, for whom Mass attendance is no longer a practice, still turn to God in prayer at least once weekly. This suggests an openness to something other than materially-focused and self-interested lives, an openness to the transcendent.

It's also true that many families continue to link with the Church at special moments in their lives, through baptism, First Holy Communion and Confirmation, and at death. This presents the Church with both the challenge and the opportunity to reach out to these families, most of whom are not regular Church-goers.

There are others for whom participation in the Christian Community at local level gives them a sense of connection and belonging.[207] Those who are part of small group with experiences of prayer, meditation, *lectio divina* and so on, frequently report that these group experiences nourish a greater sense of God in their lives. They frequently distinguish between their sense of distance from the institutional Church and the belonging they experience in their local parish community.

[207] I am grateful to Sr Patricia Greene and Sr Rita Corry for these findings from an unpublished survey carried out among parishioners in Nenagh Parish, Co Tipperary.

This is the context in which the proposed synodal process must discern ways forward. This reality may appear bleak, but it is necessary to try to name the truth of our situation if we are to have any hope of addressing it.

Learning from Previous Experiences of Listening

In Irish Dioceses over the past 10-15 years there have been many instances of diocesan processes aimed at identifying pastoral priorities and developing pastoral plans in their respective dioceses. Dioceses such as Down and Connor, Kerry, Kilmore, Ardagh and Clonmacnoise, Killaloe and more recently Cashel and Emily and likely many others have engaged in processes aimed at involving as many people as possible. The Diocese of Limerick instituted a more formal synodal process. Broadly speaking, these processes have a number of stages.

The first stage is that of listening to people and priests on the ground. Different methodologies have been employed by different dioceses, including diocesan assemblies with designated parish representatives, survey work (in some cases online surveys), local gatherings of people involved in pastoral councils/pastoral area councils, or other forms of ministry, parish groups who gather for conversation, focus groups involving constituencies whose voices would usually not be heard.

Following on from the period of listening, an analysis of what people have said is needed. Large scale listening processes require the involvement of people with skills in data analysis so that an accurate and reliable understanding of what people are saying emerges. The outcome of this analysis is the identification of key themes from what has been heard.

Once themes are identified and presented to those who were involved in the listening part of the process, a period of discernment is entered into. What is God saying to us in what we have heard? What is the Gospel call in our reality? To what pastoral priorities is the Spirit calling us? The identification of pastoral priorities is generally followed by the drafting of a Pastoral Plan, which is then presented to the wider diocese.

There is much that is positive from these processes at local Church level. Fora have been created, which have allowed the voices of lay people to be heard. Pastoral initiatives and approaches have been identified and worked on in a systematic way, which has helped give some direction. All of this is valuable.

How do these local processes relate to the Synodal Pathway now proposed? Pastoral Development personnel in dioceses which have already had significant listening processes ask if the proposed Synodal Pathway may end up repeating what has already happened at local level. There is also concern that the length of the process, currently proposed as five years, is too long and will be impossible to sustain. Others feel that the crisis in the Irish Church requires ways forward that cannot wait five years. Others still feel that there has been sufficient listening and now practical solutions and actions are needed.

My sense is that the scale of the crisis we face as a Church is bigger than can be addressed by local dioceses working in isolation. What does it mean to be a Christian Community in an increasingly secular and materialistic society? How can the Gospel message be proclaimed meaningfully in this culture? Can we take seriously the call to social justice and to care of the environment as core parts of who we are called to be and not just the concern of small groups who are often marginal to the mainstream Church? The breakdown of the clerical model of Church requires us to reimagine how we understand ministry in our Church. What forms of ministry are needed now if Christian community is to be sustained and if the Church community is to reach out to the ambient human community?

Over the past 10-15 years, similar issues have surfaced continually, in one form or another, in listening processes in dioceses all over the country. They have to do with participation and power, with sexuality and the acceptance of different sexual orientations, with young people and their absence from Church communities, with ministry and how it is expressed, with the role of women in the Church and their absence from decision making in the structures of the Church.

Many of these issues are related to culture. There is an enormous disjunction between the worldview of a hierarchically structured, patriarchal Church and that of the surrounding culture. The Church as institution is losing its place in contemporary society, I suggest, because its structures and ways of operating are alienating for those whose worldview is shaped by post-modern culture. Michael Conway has written powerfully and insightfully about this disjunction.[208]

> We are witnessing a tectonic shift in our culture away from a social order that is hierarchical in its order, vertical in its structure and deferential in its dynamics. Our culture is gradually putting in place an alternative order that is horizontal, egalitarian, functional, discourse based, person centred, communitarian and so on … We are moving from a form of order that was significantly indebted to the patriarchal system to a new form of order that is based on very different principles and values.[209]

Conway goes on to say that the Church is the one institution in Europe that has resisted the deconstruction of the patriarchal worldview with its structures, its ways of operating, its power dynamics, its modes of leadership and understanding of authority. The consequence the Church suffers is the alienation of many in contemporary culture.

A line from poet Adrienne Rich comes to mind. 'There come times – perhaps this is one of them – where we have to take ourselves more seriously or die'.[210] If the synodal pathway is to address the current crisis, the issues causing alienation must be discussed and ways forward be found. Issues of structure, participation and power are not divinely ordained. They are issues we need to confront together as adult Christians.

In response to the fall-out from the sexual abuse scandals and consequent damage to the Church, the German Bishops have focused their Synodal Path on questions which they feel underlie the crisis they have experienced as a Church: 'Power and separation of powers in the Church – joint participation and involvement in the mission', 'Priestly existence today', 'Women in ministries and offices in the Church', 'Life in succeeding relationships – Living love in sexuality and partnership'.

---

208 See for example: Michael A. Conway, 'Faith-life, Church and Institution' in *The Furrow, Vol 68, (2017), 461-474.*
209 Ibid., 467.
210 Adrienne Rich, 'Transcendental Interlude' in *The Dream of a Common Language: Poems 1974-1977* (New York: W.W. Norton & Co. 1978 & 2013), 72.

This suggests a determination and courage on the part of the German Bishops to confront difficult questions. Will there be similar courage in the Irish Church? Will bishops, priests and lay people have the courage to confront together the searching issues that underlie so many of our difficulties and are alienating for so many in post-modern Ireland?

Accountability and Trust

There is also the issue of accountability. With the initiation of a process of listening comes the responsibility of ensuring that outcomes flow from the process. 'We have been through all this before and nothing happened' is not an uncommon statement in the Irish ecclesial context. When this has been the experience on the ground, it hugely damages confidence. People will not be prepared to invest themselves again without assurance that the listening process will issue in some movement forward and practical pastoral responses will flow from it.

Trust is a crucial issue here too. My experience is that trust is greatly undermined when what has been agreed by priests and people in diocesan listening and discernment processes is allowed to be ignored at parish level. The toleration by bishops of the clerical mindset, which sees the priest as the arbiter of what happens in 'his parish', is incalculably destructive of any effort to work in a synodal way. The role of episcopal leadership is holding a diocese to account for what has been agreed in synodal processes is crucial. Disillusionment sets in when there is a failure of accountability.

Who Are the Laity?

It goes without saying that the laity are not a homogenous group. However, labels typically applied to them such as progressive or conservative do not do justice to the complexities of the different theological outlooks this term includes. In his book on the identity of Catholic Parishes today,[211] Australian theologian and priest Dr Brendan Reed has developed a parish engagement scale aimed at understanding

211 Brendan Reed: *Engaging with the Hopes of Parishioners: A Systematic, Empirical and Practical Search for a Parish Engagement Scale*, (Zurich: LIT Verlag, GmbH & Co., 2018).

how Catholic parishes – and I hypothesize both parishioners and priests – see themselves in a changed cultural environment, and how would they like to see themselves in the future?[212] The typology which emerged from the study has, I believe, parallels in the Irish situation.

Reed presents four predominant types. He explores the theological emphasis of each type and examines how each sees itself in relation to the prevailing culture. The four types he identified are as follows:

a. The Convinced
b. The Devoted
c. The Consumerist
d. The Engaged

The convinced typology looks to the Church to offer certainty and security in a time of turbulence and change. They want the Church to hand on tradition and dogma, which for them is unchanging, in an uncompromising way. The devoted typology looks to the Church to provide the comfort of a strong devotional life where prayer and liturgical life are central. There is a strong emphasis on piety, with traditional devotional prayer such as the rosary, attending exposition of the Blessed Sacrament, prayer groups, etc. The consumerist type will likely try out a number of experiences of parish before they settle on one that is to their liking. Choice is a critical value for this cohort as well as meeting personal needs.

The engaged see the need to explore the meaning of faith and its contemporary expression, seeking to relate faith to the struggle for life and meaning they see around them. They see the faith tradition as needing to find new expression appropriate to the cultural context in which they live. Engaged parishioners are conscious of living in a pluralist society. They are open to dialogue with others in shaping the future of society.

---

212 Dr Reed's study was carried out in conjunction with the Pastoral Theology Unit of the Catholic University of Leuven. While the research refers to the Australian situation, some of the study was carried out in a number of Catholic Parishes in Flanders, Belgium. My experience of working on the ground suggests these categories throw light on the reality on the ground in parishes in Ireland too.

The above categorisation is not an exact mirror of reality.[213] But they do give us a framework in which to think about the category 'laity' under consideration in this paper.

It is likely that every parish has members of each of Reed's four categories.[214] For the devoted typology, the Church exists to provide Mass, sacraments and other traditional forms of piety. They are largely happy with the traditional parish and church structure once the Mass and sacraments continue to be provided. There are also strong elements of the convinced type in the Irish Church for whom certainty is the dominant value. Adherence to and passing on an unchanging tradition is paramount for this cohort. The challenge of addressing the reality of change with the convinced and devoted typologies is that many have a theological outlook and cultural mindset that looks more to the restoration of models of Church more suited to the past. Some are pessimistic too about the surrounding culture and see the Church as needing to take a defensive stance in relation to it.

For the consumerist typology, meeting their own needs is the dominant value. For example, the online streaming of liturgies enables the possibility of choosing to participate in liturgy according to one's personal preferences. It meets individual needs but requires no commitment to community or to actively participating in the Body of Christ. Yet unless we are nourished at a deep soul level, we are unable to reach out beyond ourselves. Listening to the deep soul hungers of people today is crucial.

The engaged seek expressions of faith that resonate with contemporary experience. This cohort see themselves as part of pluralist culture. They seek to relate to the wider society, to engage in an open dialogical way, recognising that the Gospel can be a source of meaning and hope in the surrounding culture. It is this cohort the Church in Ireland needs

---

213 Stephen Bevans points out that 'models are not exact mirrors of external reality. Life does not exactly replicate the model'. However, neither are the caricatures. They help us describe aspects of experience by contrasting with other aspects. See Stephen B. Bevans, *Models of Contextual Theology*, (New York: Orbis Books, 2008), 29-31.

214 Reed suggests that parishes work predominantly from one typology. In my experience the typology adopted frequently depends on that theological worldview which the ordained bring to the parish.

so badly to attract if the Synodal Process is to enable it to find a new place in Irish Society, one that is open to engagement with the wider culture. This does not mean uncritical engagement. The insights of Michael Paul Gallagher SJ on discerning the culture and the seeds of the Gospel inherent in it is a valuable resource in this regard.[215]

Listening with Openness to Conversion and Change

The Redemptorist, Cardinal Joseph Tobin CSSR, has spoken powerfully of the need for the Church 'to listen to people who have, in one way or another, been pushed to the peripheries, in a way that is open to conversion and action'.[216] He points out that the 'septic wound' of clerical abuse has been compounded by the perennial ignoring of the voices of people who have been wounded and pushed aside by the Church. In my experience, those who have been pushed to the periphery include the poor, those who question aspects of Church teaching, those who are divorced or separated, and those who identify as LGBT persons. It is often the most creative and prophetic voices who feel pushed aside. Could this be because we defend against hearing what is uncomfortable or difficult to hear?

Perhaps the blessing of listening to the voices of those on the margins is that it offers us, the Church, the possibility of conversion. It requires us to confront our blind spots and prejudices. It calls us to humility and to acknowledging our failures as a Church. Sincere humility does not simply mean being modest and unassuming. It is recognising that we have failed and need the forgiveness and mercy of others. It also calls us to change what is oppressive or unjust in our Church structures.

---

215 Michal Paul Gallagher SJ, *Clashing Symbols: An Introduction to Faith and Culture* (London: Darton, Longman and Todd, 1997). See especially Chapter 10: Discerning Culture, pp 111 – 124.

216 Cardinal Joseph W. Tobin, CSsR, 'The power of listening to the peripheries: a traumatized Church can truly embrace the Pope Francis vision and offer a witness that is more accountable to the Gospel'. Address to the Diocese of Newark, Feb. 20, 2019. See https://www.rcan.org/power-listening-peripheries-traumatized-church-can-truly-embrace-pope-francis-vision-and-offer.

Conclusion

This paper began with the call of Pope Francis to become a wholly synodal Church. It went on to describe the crisis the Irish Church is now facing and the urgency for the synodal pathway proposed by the bishops to address it. The value of a national synodal pathway, where questions and issues greater than those that can be solved locally, was named.

Previous experiences of listening, discerning and planning in local diocesan contexts were looked at and valuable learning identified along with some shortfalls from these processes. It suggested that the proposed synodal pathway needs to go deeper than these local processes, in particular by addressing the cultural assumptions which underlie many of the issues we face as a Church. It pointed to the courage required to address difficult and uncomfortable issues, without which the deep change required to address our current reality will not happen.

The latter part of the paper examined the profile of the 'laity', the different theological outlooks it encompasses, and the challenges of engaging with vastly different perspectives about what is needed for the future.

Finally, the paper suggests that listening to the voices of those who have been pushed to the periphery of our Church may be the blessing of this synodal pathway. It may call us to conversion, to recognising our blind-spots and awakening our sense of needing the mercy and forgiveness of others. Conversion will call us to change those parts of our structures which no longer speak to our culture or which are experienced as alienating.

Questions

- *The Irish Bishops' decision to embark on a national synodal pathway is situated against a backdrop of what some would call a 'Church in Crisis', a crisis which needs to be addressed immediately and not in five years' time. Is the Irish Church more in a pre-synodal rather than synodal phase? Can the Irish Church afford to wait five years before changes come about?*

- *How can the Irish Church listen more effectively to the voices of those on the periphery and undergo a conversion that will change structures which no longer speak to our culture or which are experienced as alienating?*

14

ACCOUNTABILITY AND SYNODALITY

Nuala O'Loan

Nuala O'Loan DBE is a member of the UK House of Lords. From 2000 – 2007 she was the Police Ombudsman for Northern Ireland and she currently serves as Ireland's Roving Ambassador for Conflict Resolution and Special Envoy to Timor Leste and for UNSCR 1325, Women, Peace and Security. In this chapter, Baroness O'Loan argues that honest and effective processes of accountability are essential to the Irish Church rebuilding trust. Accountability needs to become endemic at every level of the Church's life if people are to find the courage to take on responsibility for rebuilding and reshaping the Irish Church into the future.

Baroness O'Loan is a qualified solicitor. She previously held the Jean Monnet Chair in European Law at the University of Ulster and has received honorary degrees from four universities.

The announcement by Pope Francis of a process of synodality through which every member of the Church would have an opportunity to listen, to reflect and to make known their views on the three synod issues of communion, participation and mission came as a surprise to many across the world. We had grown used to listening exercises, but the concept of a global listening exercise seemed unprecedented. Given the international reach of the exercise, the complexities of culture and language and the uncertainties of what was to be expected, it became clear that the Church as a whole was embarking on a new stage of its journey. In such a situation it becomes useful to recall what our Church actually is, and to approach the issue of discernment with the faith and trust articulated by Pope Benedict XVI in his closing reflection on the years he had served the Church:

> The Lord has given us so many days of sun and of light winds, days when the catch was abundant; there were also moments when the waters were rough and the winds against us, as throughout the Church's history, and the Lord seemed to be sleeping. But I have always known that the Lord is in that boat, and I have always known that the barque of the Church is not mine but his. Nor does the Lord let it sink; it is he who guides it, surely also through those whom he has chosen, because he so wished. This has been, and is, a certainty which nothing can shake. For this reason, my heart today overflows with gratitude to God, for he has never let his Church, or me personally, lack his consolation, his light, his love.

In our discourses, our meetings, even homilies, we rarely use the word 'accountability', yet the concept of accountability is fundamental to our faith and its structures, in theory and to some extent in practice. We accept that Jesus Christ is our Redeemer and Saviour. We are called to live a life in which we reflect on and acknowledge with sorrow those parts of our lives which are not consistent with our faith: our failures, our deliberate wrongdoing, our selfishness and most of all our failure to love God and to love one another as he has loved us. We have been blessed with the sacrament of confession. We know, too, that each of us, regardless of our calling or perceived status in life, is accountable at the end of our days to God for how we have lived our lives, how we have used the talents which he gave us, how we have responded to others and to God, individually and as part of His Church.

It is in the context of 'communion, participation and mission' that all our reflections and discussions are to be focused.

Pope Francis has said that we are to, 'meet, listen, and discern'. As Cardinal Vincent Nichols said in a homily in October 2021, 'He wants us to meet with people with whom we don't often gather, especially with people who are often left out, or who feel left out. He wants us to listen from the heart as we share our journey of faith. He wants us to ponder, prayerfully, what we see as gifts of God emerging in our meetings.'

Pope Francis is also very clear about what he does not want. He says continually: 'It is not about gathering opinions, no. This is not a survey but about listening to the Holy Spirit … The first commitment,' he says, 'is to have ears, to listen.' Again, he says: 'This is not about distinguishing between majorities and minorities: a parliament does this.' Rather, he says, 'the rejected must be part of the process and we must include our miseries!'

Accountability is about openness, transparency, and being ready and willing to account for stewardship whether as an individual, as a parent, carer or guardian, priest, bishop, or even as the Pope. Accountability, because it requires openness, is key to understanding, and understanding is key to trust. Trust is fundamental to our faith – an act of faith is an act of trust. Those 'miseries' to which the Pope referred may well include the many occasions on which trust has been damaged, leaving a sense of bewilderment.

We will all be accountable for how we participate – we will have to be both very honest and very aware of our own limitations, of the 'planks in our eyes'. Fairness and respect must be visible in all our listening exercises, even when it is hard to hear what is being said.

There is a requirement too for each of us to recognize not only our individual but also our institutional accountability for our Church. In our parishes, as we contemplate our responsibilities as parish, and listen to the experiences of those who seek to share with us, we must be alert to the gentle powerful working of the Holy Spirit among us. This is a great opportunity for individual and parish growth. These meetings, like the whole process of preparing for the synod, could be occasions of healing or they could result in an experience of exclusion, a feeling of not being listened to. At all levels in our Church, we need to be willing to speak up with courage about our realities, and that ongoing need for change and reform which is necessary in any institution. We cannot just leave it to others.

What are the major challenges faced by the Church today and will the proper understanding and exercise of true accountability assist in resolving those matters? As we contemplate how we can become a Church in which there is the greatest possible communion and participation, resulting in the most effective living of the mission to which we are all called, how can accountability help?

Sitting and listening in parishes, deaneries and bishops' conferences can seem like Groundhog Day. We have been there before. This call to communion, participation and mission is core to our faith – we hear every time we leave Mass, 'Go and proclaim the Gospel'. The issues raised by those to whom we may listen may be familiar: concern about the loss of faith in modern society, the accusations of naivety and superstition when we manifest our faith in the living God, the disdain and, on occasion, contempt for organised religion such as we practice, the loss of some of the traditional ways of being Catholic in liturgy, the difficulty in persuading people to contribute actively to Church, rather than just being passive attenders at Church. It is true also that the fear of being seen as 'Gospel greedy' (as if one could ever have too much knowledge and understanding of sacred scripture) or too assertive can undermine our ability to participate, to walk in hope and to see the light which shines even in the darkness. Essential to any discernment process whether at parish, diocesan, national or synod level will be the existence and full acceptance of a conceptual understanding of who and what we are (children of God) and of why we are on this journey of listening and discernment (because the Pope has discerned that this is what we need to do at this time in the world).

There are many other issues which cause people distress and pain. They include, on occasion, the ways in which parishes function, probably inadvertently. There is always a core group of people in every parish who give without counting the cost, who are always ready to help, but to those who come as outsiders into our midst, parish can seem like a closed shop – a group of those who are in the know, to the exclusion of others who might dream of making what they might perceive as a tiny contribution. However, listened to carefully, given a little space and encouragement, they might contribute far more than the parish or they expect. This synodal pathway is an opportunity to make that space, to provide that encouragement and to wait in anticipation as the Holy Spirit moves among us.

Other problems may relate to the way in which some parishioners and clergy conduct themselves as people of influence and control in the parish. It is a very real fact that if we are to have functioning churches, we must be prepared to provide the money to pay for clergy stipends, to meet the cost of heating, lighting and maintaining the church and its associated parish centres and other buildings. These are very real costs, and they will continue to rise. In many parishes there is accountability for how parish money is spent, but not in all. When people can see that there is, as required by Canon Law, a finance committee which reports to them about how much income there is in the parish, and what the outgoings are, they may be persuaded that there is a need to be more generous to the church which is the community within which we celebrate and mark the small steps on our daily journey and the greater occasions when we baptise our babies, confess our sins, receive the Lord in the Eucharist, watch our young people enter into holy matrimony and present those who have died to the Lord, in thanks for their lives and in prayer for their immortal souls. If we live as Christians, we must be prepared to be generous, not just with our time and our energy but also with our other resources.

If we are to be accountable for the way we approach and live our mission, then we must first listen to the words of those with whom we speak – there must be an openness to hear that which may seem strange or even alien, and an ability to acknowledge that, as Church, we have not always understood properly the divine mission entrusted to us. Rather, on occasion we have been led by the mores of the day and have failed in our treatment of so many of our fellow human beings. Our approach to major issues such as justice and equality, divorce and nullity of marriage, the birth of children in circumstances other than marriage, our approach to sexuality generally, to financial probity, to other ways of living faith in God has been flawed, on occasion deeply flawed, and rather than being conduits for the love of God we have acted with hostility imposing great pain and rejection on God's children.

Great power is exercised in our Church especially by those who are ordained, because to them is entrusted the responsibility and task of decision making. It has seemed, on occasion that there is no accountability for the exercise of that power and no reason for the preservation of that power to the ordained only. Indeed, as we contemplate the tragedies of child abuse, of the way in which unmarried mothers were treated, the financial abuses of power which emerge from time to time, the betrayals of priestly vows by some of those among our clergy and bishops, all the occasions on which terrible wrong has been done, we are faced with the terrible reality that these actions have all contributed to the breakdown in trust in Church and the resultant drift away from the Church and even, where the betrayal has been greatest, to loss of faith. When Jesus talked about allowing the little children to come to him, he was surely telling us that if that which we do causes loss of faith in others, then we are responsible for that loss of faith. Responsibility and accountability go hand in hand.

Accounts of experiences of betrayal such as those described above may be very hard to listen to, and it may be asserted that these things happened in the past, but the problem is that the loss, trauma and grief experienced does not stay in the past, rather, all too often, it lurks under the surface of a life, ready to emerge when least expected and to plunge the sufferer back to that pain. As a Church, we are challenged by this reality and by the need, above all, to care.

Of course, wherever power is reposed there exists the possibility of corruption, and power is held not only by the ordained but also by lay people, particularly in the financial sphere, where they may be involved in building projects, where there may be financial investments to be managed and similar situations which give rise to the opportunity for fraud and other crime. It happens. The scandals of criminal trials such as the current Vatican trial, in which even a cardinal stands trial, the ongoing situations in which lay people, priests and bishops across the world appear charged with financial crime, all these have massive impact whether they result in the acquittal of the defendants or not. There is too the damage wrought by the perception of hard-earned money donated by ordinary people, being spent on causes for which it was not donated. There is even the very common situation in which people donate but are never told what their money is being used for. The effect of these is to reduce trust in the Church's capacity to manage its earthly affairs with probity. The consequence of that can be that donations diminish. Yet those donations, the generosity of the people of God, are critical to the Church's ability to carry out its sacred mission. Financial irregularities and fraud, like all criminality, can result in people losing faith in the Church.

People within the Church do not speak often of such matters, yet the impact is very clear. Pope Francis has made very strenuous efforts in this context within the Holy See, and there is within the church centrally a slow drift towards recognition of the need for financial accountability.

Another area which is undoubtedly a cause for concern as we embark on this journey is the fact that current Canon Law does not provide the necessary timely, and effective resolution of problems and issues which can only be resolved through Canon Law. While the process of seeking decrees of nullity of marriage has become much faster in many areas, it can still be very long for some. In addition, there continues to be a whole range of other issues in which the situation may seem uncertain, is far less speedy and in which there is a perception of procedural unfairness – where people do not feel that they are heard and have the right to challenge the evidence against them, and where people do not understand why an individual identified by the Church as having sexually abused a child has not been laicized, for example.

Particular difficulties exist for priests or religious against whom an allegation is made of sexual abuse of a minor or an adult at risk, where there is no evidence to bring any form of criminal prosecution, and the matter is returned to the Church to be dealt with. If a canonical preliminary investigation is established, the case will almost inevitably end up before the CDF, where the detail of the procedures is some-what opaque, and the lack of resources to deal with such matters re-sults in inordinate and extraordinary delays.

There are no processes within the Church that are similar to those applicable in professions such as teaching, nursing and medicine, where although a person will have to stop working pending investiga-tion, the processes move much more swiftly and there is no necessity to move from home, as often happens in the case of accused clergy. Over 25 years have elapsed since modern systems for investigating and handling complaints were established. There are processes within the Church for training about child abuse, for preventative activity, for enhanced communications about the risks of abuse, for receiving complaints and initial management thereof, prior to either prosecu-tion and conviction or to a finding of no case to answer in law, and there are processes for identifying and managing any risk associated with an individual. However, if a case moves from the civil law into canonical investigation, the accused and the accuser will know that it will be an even longer time before there is any resolution of the mat-ters. It is unfortunately true that, on occasion, the burden of awaiting resolution of such matters can become so onerous that a person's men-tal health is affected, and that there have been suicides.

For the families and friends of all those affected by such matters the Church's handling of the process, and particularly the delays inherent therein, can become a cause for great disillusionment and ultimately for people to become disaffected and even to abandon the Church.

Matters such as these are, again, rarely spoken about in public meet-ings in the Church. We have seen, in inquiries and the media, some of the realities, yet there is a perception that this is matter which is incapable of resolution. Yet, that is not necessarily the case. Following recent recommendations for reform in this area, the Catholic Church in England and Wales is establishing a new National Tribunal Service, which will address the canonical matters connected to clergy disci-pline and canonical offences. It will exercise jurisdiction exclusively in the canonical forum, although its competence will not be limited simply to the role of adjudication. Its operational activity will extend to preliminary case evaluation as well as formation in professional regulatory procedures, evidence and other matters of canonical penal law (substantive and procedural). This will provide confidence that published standards are being upheld, and offers the possibility of enhanced impartiality, transparency and decision making in line with the practice of other professional regulatory bodies.

The theology and philosophy of our Church has developed over the millennia as we have grown in knowledge of how we exist and who we are as God's people. This specific opportunity for listening and discernment may take the Church into discussions on matters with which many would prefer not to engage.

There are those matters, on which some have said there is no possibility of change, such as the ordination of women. There are also issues such as the proposal for the abolition of the celibacy requirement for ordination. Current rules are undoubtedly the product of prayer and discernment over centuries, yet we cannot rule out the fact that we may be being led into a new dimension in which these things can and should change. In matters such as these, it will be essential that there is acute listening, listening which is sensitive to the murmurings of the Holy Spirit in each heart, and it must be borne in mind always that those who speak and call for different ways, with which we may not agree, may actually be right. Discernment can be a difficult process, particularly when we are called to discern matters which cause us discomfort or unease.

Bishops and those who are responsible for the ongoing stages of this synodal process will be aware of the need to create the kind of listening situations in which issues such as this can be raised, rather than simply refusing to engage and thereby enabling the current slow drift of people away from the Church, for reasons which are preventable.

We cannot predict what this synodal process may bring. The way in which we conduct ourselves during the process will be instrumental in our final ability to discern the best possible way forward as Church. We know that as we participate in it, we are accountable for our responses to each other in our Church, and to God. I have come to realise too, that the ways of God are not predictable and that the Holy Spirit will enlighten, warm and hearten us on the process and lift up our eyes to greater understanding, greater selflessness and greater love if we but listen.

Questions

- Some of what we hear during the listening exercises of the synodal process may be difficult to hear. What are the major challenges faced by the Church today, in Ireland and globally?

- Pope Francis has said, 'the rejected must be part of the process and we must include our miseries'. How can we ensure that all who need to be heard are listened to with fairness and respect?

15

HIERARCHICALISM AND ITS IMPLICATIONS FOR A SYNODAL STYLE OF GOVERNANCE

Patrick Treacy

Patrick Treacy is a Senior Counsel who holds a LL.M from University College London specialising in procedural law and alternative dispute resolution. He is the author of 'What Happened to Marriage'? (Catholic Truth Society, 2018) and together with his family, since 2000, has facilitated Integritas, a Domestic Centre of Christian Faith, at their home in Kilkenny, Ireland. He has widespread experience of voluntary service to Church bodies and in this essay details the challenges to synodality that arise from hierarchicalism in the Catholic Church as evidenced in corporate governance.

In recent decades in Britain and Ireland, there has been an increasing reliance by clergy and by the hierarchy upon the corporate entity of a company limited by guarantee, a 'CLG', in order to manage diocesan or congregational assets and properties. The established practice is that the CLG also obtains charitable status and is duly registered as a company and as a charity with the bodies which register companies and charities respectively. When we consider whether the new movement for synodality in the Catholic Church will lead to real and beneficial change, the manner in which the hierarchy, the clergy and the laity have conducted themselves in relation to this widespread use of the status of CLGs and charities is particularly telling for three reasons.

The first reason is that diocesan or congregational assets, which are held by a CLG and a charity, are no longer simply subject to the discipline of canon law or to the law of equity and trusts. CLGs and charities must comply with the statutory requirements of company and charity law and their respective regulatory bodies. Accordingly, the manner in which the business of a CLG and charity is conducted when managing diocesan assets, reveals the respect, or otherwise, of those members of the Catholic Church who are involved in them for the values of transparency and accountability, as these are essential objects of company and charity regulation.

The second reason is that a director of a CLG, who is simultaneously a trustee of a charity, is obliged to act in accordance with his or her fiduciary duty to the company and charity. This means that the director or charity trustee must always act in good faith in vindicating the interests of the company and charity. The concept of fiduciary duty emanates from the importance of guarding relationships which are based upon trust and confidence. The company or charity cannot protect itself. Its welfare depends upon a relationship of trust and confidence between it and its directors and charity trustees and between them also. They must be free from all pressures, including clerical or hierarchical concerns, particularly when a conflict of interest arises between that of the CLG and charity and that of a diocese. If a director and charity trustee of a company and charity, managing diocesan or congregational assets, finds that one's fiduciary duty to it is being undermined by clerical or hierarchical control, such as the deliberate and repeated withholding of information, this amounts to a complete contradiction of synodality.

The third reason is that the board of directors or charity trustees should comprise people who have a proven expertise and competency in how to realise the objects of the CLG and charity. The board of directors or charity trustees should be chosen because their spheres of competency coalesce with realising the objects of the company and charity. They also need to be allowed to exercise their competency. Accordingly, if a professional person is a director or charity trustee of a diocesan or congregational entity and finds that his or her competency is not being relied upon, or worse still, that this competency is being deliberately avoided or even undermined, through the deliberate withholding of information or otherwise, it reveals a clerical or hierarchical mindset which is the antithesis of synodality. Furthermore, if a professional allows his or her professional competence to be bypassed or undermined because of clerical or hierarchical deference, it discloses an obsequiousness and cowardice which erodes the presence of synodality within the Church.

The purpose of this article is to propose, by reference to how members of the clergy and the hierarchy, together with the laity, have behaved as directors of CLGs and charity trustees, that the project of synodality, as currently envisioned in the Catholic Church, is certain to fail. This is because it is based upon a hierarchical, canonical structure of governance which operates against proper and open dialogue and shared responsibility between the clergy, the hierarchy and the laity. This pessimistic assertion is based upon how diocesan and congregational entities in Catholicism are operated against the requirements of openness, transparency and fiduciary independence which are fundamental requirements in the correct governance and functioning of CLGs and charities. The essence of the problem, the antithesis of synodality, is further proposed to be hierarchicalism or more specifically, the manifestly contradictory nature of 'hierarchical synodality' which is what currently exists within the Catholic Church and which is a counterfeit, a subterfuge of what synodality in the Church is truly meant to be.

This article concludes with another proposal, which is that true synodality in the Catholic Church must emanate from a return to understanding the incomparable importance and centrality of the sacrament of marriage and of the family based upon it. This is because the Christian vision of marriage sets before us the ideal of what a loving, permanent, dignified and respectful relationship between a man and a woman is. It also offers us the deepest and most lasting basis for loving relationships between parents and their children, between siblings themselves and in the wider relationships of family. In other words, the natural family, which is founded upon the sacrament of marriage and healthy and loving relationships, needs to be reclaimed as the exemplar of how the Catholic Church should model all of the relationships in its life and realise the true understanding of synodality.

The counterfeit and current inevitability of hierarchal synodality.

I. What is 'hierarchical synodality'?

On the 1st of May 2020, the Australian Catholic Bishops Conference and the Catholic Religious of Australia published a report and recommendations on the governance and management of dioceses and parishes of the Catholic Church in Australia. It defined synodality as follows:

> Synodality involves the active participation of all members of the Church in its processes of discernment, consultation and co-operation at every level of decision-making and mission.[217]

This report was prepared in response to an earlier government mandated Royal Commission report charged with investigating institutional responses to allegations and incidents of child sexual abuse and related matters. The Royal Commission report called on the Catholic Church to address a series of problems, principal among them being the systemic, institutional failures in Church governance and management structures. The Royal Commission found:

> The powers of governance held by individual diocesan bishops and provincials are not subject to adequate checks and balances. There is no separation of powers, and the executive, legislative

---

217 'The Light from the Southern Cross, Promoting Co-Responsible Governance in the Catholic Church in Australia', Section 5.2.3. Ecclesial governance in the global Church, Synodality, 43.

and judicial aspects of governance are combined in the person of the pope and in diocesan bishops. Diocesan bishops have not been sufficiently accountable to any other body for decision-making in their handling of allegations of child sexual abuse or alleged perpetrators.[218]

This lack of accountability in the Catholic Church feeds a culture of 'hierarchicalism', a term defined by James Keenan S.J.[219] In reflecting upon the continuous cover-up of the sexual abuse crisis in the Catholic Church, he names the real source of this crisis, being the episcopal culture of hierarchicalism in all 'its brutality and profound lack of accountability'.[220] Hierarchicalism is an insidious force that works for evil in the Church. It undermines accountability and transparency. It is the antithesis of synodality.

Hierarchicalism refers to that sense of entitlement a bishop may have and may share with other members of the episcopate. It is a denial of responsibility and an addiction to authority. It is a dark spirit of control and an absence of the humility that comes from continuous acts of genuine service and care to others. It seeks to conceal and then resorts to lies. It feigns interest in, and concern for, the wounded, but beneath this insincere and superficially smiling visage lies a heart that is corrupted by conceit, craving clerical and public recognition as the cancer of ambition for advancement within the Church takes an ever increasing root. It pretends to listen and is fed by the obsequious practice of others who pretend to speak. It commits the one sin our Lord showed no tolerance for – hypocrisy. This hypocrisy thrives within a system without transparency and accountability. Hierarchicalism always tends to defend and perpetuate itself. It despises external criticism or controls. It constantly deflects from external regulation and remains unhindered in its growth within an internal culture of deference and preservation of shared status.

---

218 Royal Commission into Institutional Responses to Child Sexual Abuse, 15 December 2017, Final Report, Volume 16(2), 681.

219 James F. Keenan SJ, *Vulnerability and Hierarchicalism* Melita Theologica, Journal of the Faculty of Theology, University of Malta, 68/2 (2018): 129-142.

220 Ibid., 135.

Hierarchical synodality is a term used to describe how hierarchical-ism operates to create the pretence of the hierarchy genuinely listening to others, to be 'journeying' with them or sharing in their suffering, when, in truth, the underlying and controlling intent is to preserve the existing hierarchical status and structures of authority within the Church. It is characterised by an obsession with secrecy. In the context of corporate and charity governance, it finds its expression when a bishop is the chair of a board meeting of directors and charity trustees, when he listens to all of the other members of the board with an appar-ent interest and concern and with a regular smile. When the meeting concludes, however, he then proceeds to follow his own agenda for the organisation or entity in question without the slightest regard to what his fellow directors and charity trustees have previously suggested or advised. With hierarchical synodality at work in the organisation, the directors and charity trustees will have had essential communications withheld from them before the meeting chaired by the bishop com-mences. Similarly, he will withhold key information from them in the aftermath of their meeting. Such a bishop has no regard for board members' fiduciary obligations in corporate and charities law or for the fact that they are undermined in acting as fiduciaries by virtue of him withholding essential information from them.

Hierarchicalism, by its very nature, can never be synodal. It is the antithesis of what synodality is. Accordingly, the term 'hierarchical syn-odality' is not simply an oxymoron in which apparently contradictory terms appear in conjunction. It is entirely contradictory in its essence because it is built on 'them' and 'us', on an elite and the common, on the insiders and the uninformed, on the educated and the ignorant. Hierarchical synodality gives the deceptive appearance of these two con-stituencies appearing to consult with each other when, in practice, the former of each coupling always dismisses the latter. By reason of its inherently contradictory nature, it is built to fail because it is founded upon an elitist vision of vocation as the exercise of power rather than as service to be given. It gives the appearance of listening and generates a false sense of belonging to a group. Yet, this falsity is invariably revealed because hierarchical synodality proceeds on the lie that it can find all the answers and that it is unanswerable to any external authority.

II. Episcopal malpractice in company and charities law

By turning to the legal regulation of companies and charities, one can clearly see how hierarchical synodality operates in practice. In Irish law, section 228 of the Companies Act 2014 provides a statement of the principal fiduciary duties of the directors of a CLG. These include not agreeing to restrict the director's power to exercise an independent judgment unless this is expressly permitted by the company's constitution, is necessary for a transaction or engagement to be entered into which is in the interests of the company, or where the director is otherwise released from this obligation. The director must be independent of all hierarchical control and interference which could interfere with vindicating the interests of the CLG, as a person who owes a fiduciary duty to it.

Nonetheless, a practice of which I am aware is of a bishop establishing a CLG, with charitable status, to control diocesan assets, having three directors, being the bishop himself and two vicars general of his diocese. This is fundamentally contrary to the requirements of the Companies Act 2014 and, in turn, the law relating to charities, that a director and charity trustee exercises independent judgment in the exercise of his or her duties to the company and charity. The constriction upon the independence of a vicar general, acting as a director or charity trustee, arises by reason of Canon 480 of the Code of Canon Law of the Catholic Church. It provides that:

> A vicar general and an episcopal vicar must report to the diocesan bishop concerning the more important affairs which are to be handled or have been handled, and they are never to act contrary to the intention and mind of the diocesan bishop.[221]

A vicar general is mandated, therefore, by canon law *never* to act contrary to the intention and mind of his diocesan bishop. When a bishop arranges for his vicar general to act as a director of a CLG and

---

221 1983 Code of Canon Law Title III. *The Internal Ordering of Particular Churches.* (Cann. 460 – 572), Chapter II. The Diocesan Curia Art. 1 Vicars General and Episcopal Vicars. Canon 480.

as a charity trustee, he orchestrates the engagement of a person who is divested of the capacity to exercise independent judgment and thereby canonically constrained from vindicating the interests of the company and charity over those of the bishop. This is episcopal malpractice because it frustrates the fiduciary duty of a director and a charity trustee. It is a manifestation of hierarchical synodality. It goes unnoticed and uncriticised in the Catholic Church because of hierarchicalism. It is an insult to the true spirit of synodality.

III. The clericalisation of the laity

A lay Catholic is called to be loyal to the Church. This loyalty is meant, in turn, to be an expression of the deepest fidelity to Jesus Christ and to a lived faith in, and commitment to, the persons of the Holy Trinity. This should entail a corresponding support for the episcopate. It may also entail a direct challenge to someone with episcopal authority. Many lay Catholics automatically assume that loyalty to a bishop is a fail safe way of being faithful to the Church. It is no such thing. Lay Catholics are invariably called to journey away from a bishop so as to ensure that they are agents for integrity within the Church. The laity, the clergy and the hierarchy are meant to be people of God who are attentively walking together, as opposed to ecclesial categories of Catholics who are sleep walking together, drugged by the insidious nature of hierarchical narcissism into an unthinking disposition of clerical deference.

This is made manifest by laity who are satisfied simply with the pretence of being listened to by clergy and the hierarchy because it soothes their own insecurity by being given a parochial significance. The laity who behave in this way need local esteem and recognition but they offer nothing other than an obstacle to the Church expressing the vision of the Gospels. Mark Slatter, when writing about the nature of clerical culture, named the culture which creates this co-dependent, mutually narcissistic dynamic as follows:

> A culture is a network of personal meaning and valuing. Clerical culture hinges on leaders attracting similarly disposed persons through the laws of social attraction, evoked in different ways since Plato as the principle of "like seeks after like". The

psychology engenders webs of kinship among priests, bishops and similarly disposed lay groups, bishops and cardinals, wealthy lay Catholics and think tanks. They always find each other through family resemblance, whatever that happens to be.[222]

The understanding of synodality which is currently operative in the Catholic Church actually works against the realisation of integrity within it. The essential reason for this is because this understanding of synodality allows the cancer of hierarchicalism to metastasise in the body of the Church in all of its narcissistic forms. It offers a false promise of truthful listening and honest speech between the laity and the episcopate, which is continuously undermined by the hierarchical culture which runs through the spinal column of governance in the Catholic Church. For this reason, the health of the Catholic Church demands one thing, before all else, in the conduct of the laity. It is to move from the culture of obsequiousness, endemic in the relationship between the laity and the episcopate, to the foreign and uncharted territory of rigorous personal integrity in one's interactions with those in positions of ecclesial responsibility.

IV. The corresponding exclusion of the laity from their own competencies

Another dynamic which undermines synodality is the deliberate frustration of lay people exercising their gifts and relying upon their experience on behalf of the Church. In these situations, there are often highly professional people involved who want to help the Church on a voluntary basis. These people have great demands upon their time. They are independent. They have no interest in some pretence of being listened to. In fact, they detest this charade. Such persons are deeply threatening, however, to the culture of hierarchicalism. It demands that they have to be controlled through having information, to which they are entitled, withheld from them. When they challenge a culture of hierarchicalism, they are demonised and accused of being

---

222 Mark Slatter, 'Clerical Crisis: Flock and Pasture Can't Tell Shepherd Who He is', National Catholic Reporter (11 March 2019).

calumnious of the member of the hierarchy whose control is being subjected to their independent, professional scrutiny.

This pseudo-engagement of lay professionals by the hierarchy and the ensuing façade of hierarchical synodality is seen in the application of Canon 492 of the Code of Canon Law of the Catholic Church.[223] It provides that dioceses are required to have a Finance Council. At least three members of the faithful are required to be on the Finance Council for a five-year term. The bishop or his delegate presides over it. The three lay members are appointed by the bishop. Persons who are related to the bishop up to the fourth degree of consanguinity or affinity are excluded from the Finance Council. They prepare the annual diocesan budget, examine the annual report on income and expenses, provide counsel on investments and the hiring of financial officers, as well as performing other duties.

The bishop, according to church law, can delegate authority but not responsibility. In other words, the sole responsibility of the bishop for financial matters in his diocese requires that exclusive authority remains with him. The problem with this, however, is the absence of account-ability. Accountability in church law is aimed upward and inward in the hierarchy and not downward and outward to the laity. This is the understanding of 'accountability' operative in hierarchical synodality.

As seen in the workings of Canon 492, it appears to involve con-sultation between the hierarchy and the laity but it is not a meeting of equals, of those who are co-responsible for the financial welfare of the diocese, any more than that of a King with his courtiers in the Middle Ages. The bishop chairs all meetings. The bishop decides who his consulters are. The bishop retains full power. The bishop is only accountable within an internal hierarchical structure. He has no real accountability unless reported to an external regulatory body by someone whom he has usually been instrumental in appointing to assist him in his diocese. Someone who is canonically or contractual-ly obligated to a bishop will invariably avoid recourse to an external body to seek regulation of his conduct.

223 1983 Code of Canon Law Title III. *The Internal Ordering of Particular Churches*, (Cann. 460 – 572), Chapter II. The Diocesan Curia Art. 3 The Finance Council and The Finance Officer, Canon 492.

Allied to this, while the Finance Council gives an appearance of synodality in relation to the conduct of the financial affairs of the diocese, the bishop can avail of the structure of a CLG and make his vicar general a fellow director, that is a supposed fiduciary, exercising independent judgment. As noted earlier, the vicar general is then required by Canon 480 'never to act contrary to the intention and mind of the diocesan bishop'. This is hierarchical synodality. It is untruthful. It is corrupting. It has nothing of the vision of the Gospels.

V. The characteristics of hierarchical synodality

The problem with the systematic exclusion of the laity from their own competencies is that their truthful, synodal engagement with the clergy and the hierarchy is not only lost but the cancer of hierarchicalism cannot be challenged or even named. A closeted culture of deference between the hierarchy and the laity makes the articulation of truth subordinate to not discommoding or even questioning each other. This leads to the cognitive dissonance of hierarchical synodality because it cannot see itself in its own narcissistic mirror. The sort of transparent characteristics of hierarchical synodality which are seldom acknowledged, let alone named, are:

* The knowing and wilful withholding of information, correspondence and communications by a bishop from others who cannot exercise a specific competency properly without this information;

* The engagement of unnecessary and wasteful professional assistance, which is engaged so as to provide a protective ring around the bishop and fend off those both within and outside of the entity or organisation who have legitimate criticisms to make of how he has conducted its affairs;

* The calling upon a person with expertise or power within an entity or organisation to assist the bishop in relation to issues unrelated to it, primarily for the purpose of developing a sense of misplaced loyalty or affinity between the bishop and that person so as the former can retain control within it;

- The emergence of a group within a group, an internal hierarchicalism of secrecy, whereby the bishop shares certain information with an inner and uncritical circle within an entity or organisation when all of the members of the group are not only entitled to this information but require it to exercise their competencies properly;

- The selection of persons who are either canonically or contractually obligated to the bishop, or who have shown a need to be deferential to the bishop for their own parochial recognition and aggrandisement, so as to create a continuous majority or even unanimity in support of his views as to how matters should be conducted within an entity or organisation, even when these persons are required by law to exercise independence in their engagement with that bishop in order to vindicate its interests as its fiduciaries;

- The continuous reliance upon the majority of unquestioning supporters even when this reliance has been advised by the minority, who have the necessary expertise, that the obsequious, uncritical support of the majority is incompatible with legal requirements and theologically and spiritually indefensible;

- The ascribing of false motives to anyone who raises a question, let alone a criticism, of how the bishop is conducting the affairs of the entity or organisation;

- The grandiose myopia of a bishop who denies that he could have any conflict of interest in how he conducts all of the affairs of his diocese because the apparently conflicting interests are all part of a grand project which everyone else, working for the good of diocese, under his leadership, should be aware of;

- The treatment of the management of safeguarding within the diocese as the sole test of good governance to the detriment of all other issues of governance whether financial, managerial, charitable, educational or otherwise;

- A fracturing of relationships with the theologians and canonists who question the spiritual, theological or canonical integrity of the bishop's conduct or who raise questions in relation to the bishop's governance or ways of proceeding;

- The use of prayer at meetings in a manner that is superficial, saccharine or spiritually manipulative and which is designed to inhibit or subvert the exercise of independent thought;

- The absence of joy or inspiration in the leadership which the bishop provides to the organisation or entity with an ennui, an irritation, a restlessness and an impatience manifesting in his attitude and conduct;

- A desire for public attention and approval, which conceals an underlying and marked hypocrisy in relation to the subject being publicly discussed, coupled with a studied avoidance of engagement in the defence of Church teaching which is controversial in the public square;

- A continuous undermining of priests, deacons, religious or theologians who are not robotic in their support of the bishop, so as to ensure that these critics do not obtain further authority in any context in the Church, which would strengthen their voices as critics of his and of the absence of integrity in his approach.

VI. 'Hierarchical synodality' guarantees clericalism

When commenting upon hierarchicalism, James Keenan SJ has also made the following observation:

> We now see how the hierarchical culture has exercised its power and networking capabilities in the cover-up of their own actions. What we are only beginning to see is that hierarchicalism and its lack of accountability and ability to act with impunity will be harder to dismantle than clericalism and in fact will

guarantee the survival of clericalism, for the former is the father and promoter of the second.[224]

This statement is chilling in its observation that hierarchicalism will be harder to dismantle than clericalism and that the former *guarantees* the survival of the latter. What this means, in effect, is that any process that advances synodality cannot be allowed to feed the cancer of hierarchicalism. The false listening, which is the defining characteristic of hierarchicalism, brings all of its falsity to life in a process that claims to be synodal but yet is rigidly hierarchical in practice. For a synodal process to have integrity, therefore, it must be based upon a model of the Church which does not dismantle the hierarchy but which places it on the periphery, in a place of humble service of another institution of Christian and Catholic life, which exemplifies the true meaning of synodality, being at its centre.

Synodality founded upon the sacrament of marriage and the family based upon it

It is clear from the sober reality of how some CLGs and charities are being misused in the management and control of diocesan and congregational assets, through the endemic and insidious nature of hierarchical synodality, that the project of finding true synodality in the governance of the Catholic Church requires a radically different approach. The use of the term 'radical' is twofold. This alternative approach must be radically different from the pomp and self-aggrandisement of hierarchical synodality. It must also involve a return to the very root, the *radix* of the Church, to its spiritual foundation and historical origins.

I. Synodality as a style to be adopted

When addressing the leaders of the French Catholic Action movement at the Vatican on the 13th of January 2022, Pope Francis said that the synodal process is a path of engagement that makes room for the Holy Spirit, and not a 'majority consensus like a parliament' to

224 Address of His Holiness Pope Francis to the delegation of the Catholic Action Movement of France, Clementine Hall, Thursday, 13 January 2022.

guide the universal church. He said that synodality is 'not a plan or a programme to be implemented' but 'a style to be adopted' that listens to the spirit through the word of God, prayer and adoration' (8).

The emphasis by Pope Francis upon synodality as a 'style' reflects a major theme of Vatican II identified by John O'Malley SJ in his seminal text bearing this name.[225] It refers to a rhetorical shift from the juridical, legislative style of the canon, which characterised previous councils, to a panegyric style, a public pronouncement of an idealised portrait of the Catholic Church, a vision of Catholicism aimed at inspiring admiration and appropriation. In this regard, it is of note that Vatican I was the first council in the history of the Church to exclude the laity from participation. While Vatican II called forth a new synodal style from where the Church can radiate the vitality of the Gospels, hierarchical synodality kills this objective. A truly synodal style must be found elsewhere. When we listen to the Spirit through the Word of God, prayer and adoration, the central question arises as to where can we see this synodal style, this way of journeying together.

I. The synodal style of marriage and the family

We find this synodal style at the beginning of the New Testament. We see it in the journeying together, the synodal path, of Mary and Joseph to Bethlehem as they prepare for the birth of Jesus. We see it in the shepherds journeying together and finding Mary and Joseph and the child lying in a manger. We see it in the journey, and the adoration, of the Magi before the child. We see it in the Holy Family journeying to Egypt and remaining there until the death of Herod. The synodal style is not in these mutual journeys *per se*. It is in the relationship that binds these people as they go in search of God, as they live for God and as they live and relate within the ambit of divine love.

We see it in the Acts of the Apostles, in the meetings of the early followers of Jesus in each other's homes. We see it in the homes of married couples, united in their emerging belief as to who Jesus really is, opening their homes as places of gathering and worship, in the midst of Roman oppression of Christians. This is the historical

225 John W. O'Malley SJ, *What Happened At Vatican II* (2010) Belknap Press.

foundation of the Church. This is the foundational structure of synodality – marriage, family, households, friendship and faith.

The life-long union of a man and woman, consciously founded upon
God's love is *the* place of true synodality. For this reason, the best starting point for the Catholic Church now in discerning the style of synodality is to deepen the understanding of *Amoris Laetitia*, the Apostolic
Exhortation of Pope Francis of 2016 on love in the family. When marriage and the family founded upon it are placed at the rightful centre as the key institution that nourishes Christian faith, only good can
come from this – the mutual respect and care between men and wom-
en, the synergy that arises from the dignity of their complementarity,
their shared commitment as parents and educators of their children,
the growth of children in the ambit of love from their parents and their
relatives and friends, the building of bonds of solidarity between families and the emergence of greater cohesion in society and solidarity with
those who are impoverished, vulnerable and excluded.

One of the key revelations throughout the most stringent period of
the imposition of the Covid-19 lockdown restrictions was how important the family home is as the place of Church. When liturgies were suspended and Churches were closed, countless families watched the Mass
being televised and particularly, the Masses celebrated by Pope Francis
from the chapel at the Domus Sanctae Marthae in the Easter period of
2020. This experience of families renewing the practice of prayer and liturgical engagement in their own homes reflected the deepest truth that
the most beautiful style of synodality is founded upon the Christian
truth of sacramental marriage and the natural family.

The Christian home, the domestic church, which is an authentic
place of love and care, a sanctuary, a school, a shelter, a sign and ultimately, a place of lived stability in love and relationships, is the place
where the true meaning of synodality flourishes. What the recognition of this truth would mean in reality for the structures of governance within the Catholic Church is that the clergy and the episcopate would constantly take their lead from these families, seeking to
serve them and listen to them in the most genuine and sincere manner
possible when discerning the future direction of the Church. In turn,
these families would also see that the deepest friendships with the

clergy and with the episcopate are essential to their welfare as married couples and as families. Those in ordained and religious life would be consulted with, and relied upon, as family friends and supporters who constantly enable the family to remain located within, and an image of, the love of the persons of the Holy Trinity. For as Pope Francis stated at the beginning of *Amoris Laetitia*, 'the triune God is a communion of love, and the family is its living reflection'.[226]

This calls for a new understanding of the inter-relationship of the sacramental life of marriage and of the ordained and consecrated in the life of the Catholic Church. It entails a movement away from the false centrality of hierarchical synodality to the living cells of marriage and family life. It requires a simple but profound relocation of where we understand that the centre of the reform of the Catholic Church must be based. It has to be centred upon sacramental marriage and the natural family. Synodality must emerge from the integrity of marriage and the bonds of family kinship and can only be betrayed by the existing hypocrisy and falsity of hierarchical synodality.

Questions

- *To what extent does hierarchical synodality exist in your diocese; have you ever been complicit in it and if so, what was that like?*

- *What awareness and knowledge do you have of structures of corporate governance in your diocese?*

- *Treacy claims here that the family is the place of true synodality; do you agree and how might this influence the approach to synodality in your diocese?*

---

226 Post-Synodal Apostolic Exhortation *Amoris Laetitia* of the Holy Father Francis to Bishops, Priests and Deacons, Consecrated Persons, Christian Married Couples and all the lay faithful on love in the family (19 March 2016), 11.